DESIGN & THE DECORATIVE ARTS

VICTORIAN BRITAIN 1837-1901

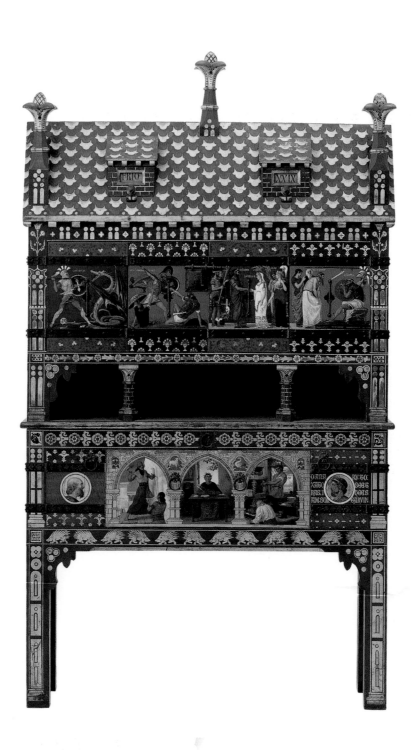

DESIGN & THE DECORATIVE ARTS

VICTORIAN BRITAIN 1837-1901

Michael Snodin and John Styles

V&A Publications

First published by V&A Publications, 2004

V&A Publications
160 Brompton Road
London SW3 1HW

Originally published as part of
Design and the Decorative Arts: Britain 1500–1900, 2001

Designed by Janet James

ISBN 1 85177 422 X

A catalogue record for this book is available from the British Library.

Front cover illustration: Sideboard, 1867–70. Designed by Edward William Godwin. VAM Circ.38–1953.
Back cover illustration: Sewing machine, 1875–92. Designed and manufactured by Edward Ward. VAM Loan: Science Museum 101.
Frontispiece: Cabinet, 1858. Designed by William Burges. VAM Circ.217–1961.
Contents page: Clock, 1896–1901. Designed by C. F. A. Voysey. VAM W.5–1998.

Printed in Italy

V&A Publications
160 Brompton Road
London SW3 1HW
www.vam.ac.uk

Contents

Acknowledgements

Planning, writing and editing this book and its companion volumes was an integral part of the wider British Galleries project at the V&A. As the book's editors and principal authors, we owe a great debt of gratitude to Christopher Wilk, who led the British Galleries project, Alan Borg, former Director of the V&A, Gwyn Miles, Director of Projects & Estate, and to all the staff of the project, in particular to Karen Livingstone, in her role as the Victorian Gallery Team Co-ordinator.

For ideas, references and advice on illustrations we are grateful to Cathy Arbuthnot, Philip Atkins, Elizabeth Bonython, Quintin Colville, Richard Edgcumbe, Clive Edwards, Hazel Forsyth, Anthony Kersting, Sarah Medlam, Alex Werner, Michael Whiteway, the late Clive Wainwright, James Yorke and Jonathan Zeitlin, as well as to all our fellow contributors to the book. Thanks are also due to the many students on the V&A/RCA M.A. Course in the History of Design who have written relevant essays and dissertations, from which we learned much. We are grateful to Anthony Burton, Martin Daunton, Maurice Howard, Peter Mandler and Amanda Vickery for reading sections of the text and commenting on them.

We would like to thank the following people for their hard work and support: Mary Butler at V&A Publications and the team she assembled, especially project manager Geoff Barlow, copy-editor Mandy Greenfield, designer Janet James and indexer John Noble; the V&A's photographers and the staff of the V&A Picture Library; Kim Smith; Alicia Weisberg-Roberts; Paul Greenhalgh and Carolyn Sargentson.

Finally we must register our gratitude to our colleagues in the Department of Prints, Drawings and Paintings at the V&A and on the V&A/RCA M.A. Course in the History of Design, and most importantly, to our families. Thank you.

The book is dedicated to our fathers.

Michael Snodin and John Styles

Notes for Readers

For books and prints, the place of publication is London unless otherwise stated. For objects, the country of manufacture is Great Britain unless otherwise stated. Illustrations are numbered by chapter. Cross-references to illustrations take the form 3:12, the first number indicating the chapter, the second the illustration number. In the captions, h. indicates height, w. width, l. length and diam. diameter. Dimensions are provided only in those cases where the size of an object is unclear or is discussed in the text.

Foreword

This book originally appeared as the final section of *Design and the Decorative Arts: Britain 1500–1900*, the book published to complement and contextualize the Victoria & Albert Museum's new British Galleries 1500–1900, opened in November 2001. *Design and the Decorative Arts: Victorian Britain 1837–1901* now appears as a separate paperback, alongside its Tudor and Stuart and Georgian counterparts, to make the subject accessible to a wider audience.

Like the V&A's British Galleries, this book is primarily concerned with those apparently functional, but often deliberately aesthetically pleasing objects which fall between the traditional concerns of the fine arts and architecture. They include furniture, ceramics, metalwares, textiles and clothing, graphic works of various kinds, as well as the immensely varied products of manufacturing we associate with the phrase 'industrial design'. These are the objects which have come to constitute the territory of design in its most familiar modern usage.

The question of design is central to this book. The earliest meaning of the word in Britain was close to the Italian term *disegno* and was intimately linked to the activity of drawing. Thus a design was a drawing or print, and the activity of designing was to make a drawing which would enable a two- or three-dimensional object to be made, whether by hand, machine, or a combination of the two. More recently, the term design has often been used to refer exclusively to modern objects, especially those whose appearance was shaped by architects, industrial or product designers, by the tenets of twentieth-century Modernism, or the imperatives of industrial mass production. In this context the focus is on the final look of the object – its design. By contrast, historic objects like those in the V&A have been described as decorative, or applied, art. These are nineteenth-century terms which aimed to associate decorative, practical or utilitarian objects with the status of the fine arts, whilst continuing to differentiate them from it. The term decorative art, unlike applied art, still has popular currency and is therefore used in the title of this book.

Yet even before the nineteenth century, the word design could have the broader meaning of an intention, a plan, or a conception. Today it is this meaning which prevails when we use the word design in relation to objects. When we speak of an object's design we mean its overall characteristics and the processes that have taken place in order to create it. It is in this sense that the word design is employed in this book. The book identifies design as a complex and multi-layered process, including research, experimentation, manufacture, marketing and use, rather than concerning itself solely with the history of drawn or printed designs, or with the appearance of the finished object.

The V&A is Britain's National Museum of Art and Design. Its collections represent what people at various periods in the past – patrons, consumers, collectors, curators – have considered to be the best of their kind in aesthetic terms. This book, rooted as it is in the V&A's collections, reflects this history of institutional collecting. As a consequence, it deals principally with what are referred to as high-design objects. These were objects that embodied a deliberate striving after the most prized aesthetic effects of their era. They were made to be used by the economically and socially privileged whose tastes dictated what was considered beautiful and fashionable at any time. It was they who commanded the resources necessary to procure the most expensive materials and to enjoy the fruits of the most skilled techniques of manufacture. The book acknowledges that these high-design objects were only one element in the wider visual culture that prevailed in Victorian Britain, a visual culture which in many of its more everyday aspects remains poorly understood. It is able to address a wider range of objects than the British Galleries and place them in a deeper historical context. Where possible, it makes reference to everyday objects and to the people for whom and by whom they were made.

The book is organized around four distinct but complementary questions: What were the formal aesthetics of different styles? Which people and institutions led taste? How did new modes of living lead to the design of new types of objects or the increased consumption of existing ones? What was new, in terms of products, materials and techniques of manufacture? Different questions might have been asked, but these four themes would inevitably form the core of them. It is not a book about the history of Victorian Britain, although its introduction links design to that broader history. Nor is it a history of British designers, although many of them grace its pages. Rather it is a book about design in Victorian Britain. It considers what was distinctively British about British design, but it also explores the ways that 'Britishness' was constructed, more often than not, by the creative adaptation of objects and visual ideas that originated elsewhere. Britain is taken to mean the territory of Great Britain, in other words England, Scotland and Wales.

CHAPTER 1

Introduction

JOHN STYLES

1. The workshop of the world

The Great Exhibition of the Works of Industry of all Nations, held in London's Hyde Park in the summer of 1851, marked the high-water mark of British economic power. Britain in the middle of the nineteenth century was the globe's pre-eminent manufacturing nation, quite literally the workshop of the world. It commanded a far larger proportion of world trade in manufactured goods than any of its major competitor countries. Yet the Exhibition was not simply an exercise in British industrial triumphalism. Indeed, the concerns that inspired its founders, attracted its six million visitors and animated its critics reveal a combination of pride in British economic success and unease about the economic and cultural sustainability of that success, which was characteristically Victorian.

The Exhibition attracted immense audiences, ranging from the landed nobility to the more affluent, skilled sections of the working classes. More women attended than men. Many visitors – probably most – enjoyed it principally as a spectacle. It offered a gargantuan celebration of modernity, progress, civilization and internationalism, as its British organizers conceived them, enclosed within the technological wizardry of a structure made almost entirely from glass and iron – the Crystal Palace. The very fact that this, the first truly international exhibition, took place in London could hardly fail to highlight Britain's economic and technological superiority. But the Exhibition also affirmed a number of other aspects of mid-nineteenth-century British life. It provided a powerful endorsement for the British policy of peaceful international competition through free trade. It demonstrated public support for Queen Victoria and her husband, Prince Albert, who was one of the Exhibition's foremost promoters. And the good behaviour of its humbler visitors calmed fears among the comfortably-off that a resumption of the working-class political agitations of the 1840s was imminent.

1 Detail of *The Opening of the Great Exhibition by Queen Victoria on 1st May 1851*, 1851–2. By Henry Courtney Selous. Oil on canvas. VAM 329-1889.

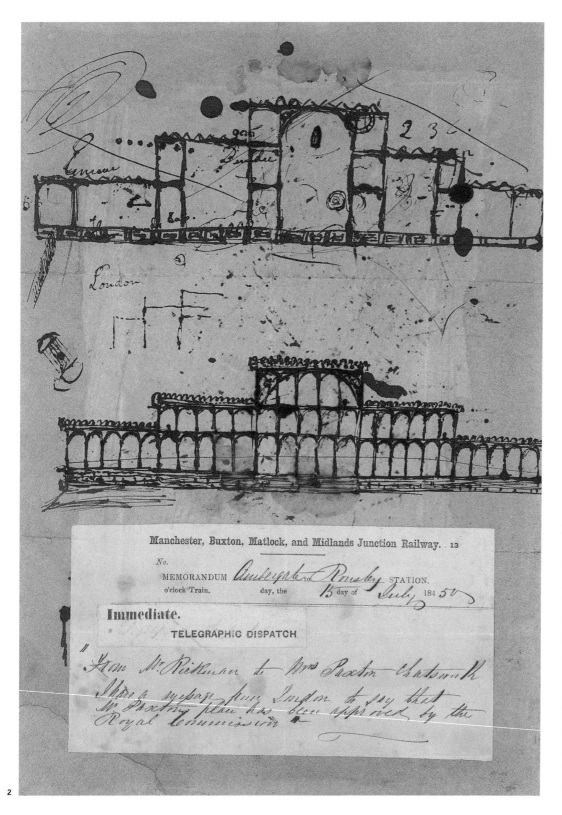

Yet alongside the overwhelming pride in British achievement and the prevailing sense of national superiority engendered by the Exhibition there were worries. One of the main reasons for holding the Exhibition had been dissatisfaction with the international competitiveness of British products, especially in the high-design sector. International competitiveness became a pressing issue for British producers as successive governments between the 1820s and the 1860s pursued the objective of free trade, dismantling the customs duties that had previously protected British-made goods from foreign imports. Those who promoted the Exhibition believed that British public taste was defective and the visual design of British manufactured goods poor. The Exhibition did not assuage their fears. Visitors seemed to be attracted to whatever was large and showy. Moreover, it was the French who displayed the most refined examples of conventional taste, winning the majority of prizes in the applied-art

2 First sketch for the Crystal Palace, 11 June 1850. By Sir Joseph Paxton. This sketch was drawn on blotting paper by the architect while he was attending a Midland Railway board meeting in Derby. It was converted into proper drawings within a week. Pen and ink on pink blotting paper, mounted on a sheet of wove paper with a telegram form. VAM E.575-1985.

categories. 'French superiority in artistic industries is no longer in doubt,' crowed one French journalist, 'even in the eyes of the English.' In machinery, where Britain was undoubtedly dominant, American, French and German technology challenged the British in a number of fields. And beyond the barrage of journalistic approval that greeted the Exhibition were heard other, more critical voices. Radicals attacked its failure to acknowledge the workers who toiled in workshop and factory to create the exhibits. Conservatives, like the writer Thomas Carlyle, contemptuous of an urban, industrial, mass society, dismissed the Exhibition as a 'congregation of empty, windy mortals'. Cultural critics, like John Ruskin, argued that artefacts made by machinery without the creative involvement of the worker could have no aesthetic value. For Ruskin, the Crystal Palace was mere technology. 'We suppose ourselves to have invented a new style of architecture,' he complained, 'when we have magnified a conservatory.'

The Victorian era was one of immense self-confidence, but it was a self-confidence sometimes assailed by doubts. Victorian Britain experienced a paradoxical alliance of material optimism and spiritual disquiet. Nowhere was this ambivalence more acute than in the field of design and the decorative arts. In the contradictory reactions to the Great Exhibition we find rehearsed the controversies – economic and social, aesthetic and moral – that were to engage designers and artists for the rest of Victoria's reign.

2. State and nation

Queen Victoria ascended the throne in 1837 at the age of 18. Her two immediate royal predecessors and uncles, the unpopular George IV and his brother William IV, had both died without surviving legitimate children. Victoria's great popularity towards the end of her reign, most obvious at the Royal Jubilees of 1887 and 1897, masks the extent to which support for the monarchy had previously waxed and waned, and, to some extent, did so throughout her reign.

Victorian Britain resembled most other European states of the period in that it was a monarchy. At the end of Victoria's reign in 1901 the vast majority of Europeans were subjects of kingdoms or empires, just as they had been at its start, more than 60 years earlier. But none of these nineteenth-century European monarchies escaped the consequences of the French Revolution of 1789. Despite the rapid demise of the revolutionary regime in France, the demands it unleashed – that each state should represent a distinct national population and that all the people of that nation should have a say in its government – were to affect Europe for the whole of the nineteenth century and beyond. In the case of France itself, these demands led eventually, in 1870, to the permanent replacement of kings and emperors by a republic. In the cases of Italy and Germany, which had for centuries been divided into a patchwork of small and medium-sized political entities, a series of wars in the 1850s and 1860s resulted in their unification as large nation states, ruled by monarchs.

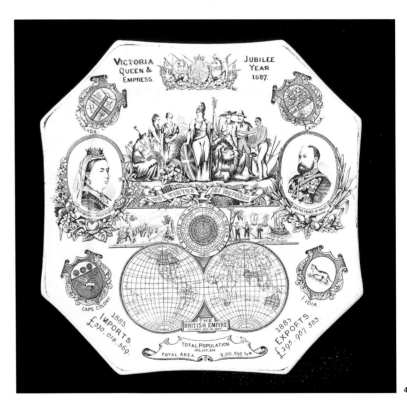

4

---

3 *France No. 3*, 1852. From *Dickinson's comprehensive pictures of the Great Exhibition of 1851*, 1854 (second edition; first published 1852). Designed by Joseph Nash; printed and published by Dickinson Brothers, London. This view shows the French section at the Exhibition. Colour lithograph with some watercolour and varnish retouching. VAM 19536:5.

4 Plate, made in 1887; design registered in 1886. Made by Wallis Gimson & Co., Lane Delph Pottery, Fenton, Staffordshire. This popular type of Golden Jubilee item was sold in Britain and exported to India and other parts of the Empire. The plate displays statistics that boast of a successful trading nation and imperial power. Earthenware, lead-glazed, transfer-printed. VAM Circ.198-1966.

QUEEN VICTORIA AND HER FAMILY

Suzanne Fagence Cooper

From the moment she ascended the throne in 1837, Queen Victoria (1837–1901) enjoyed an unprecedented hold on the public imagination. Her portrait was found in magazines and advertisements, on sheet music and, of course, on that recent innovation, the postage stamp. Her marriage to Albert, the Prince Consort, in 1840 reinforced her position and the fashionable couple patronized the arts and sciences. The Queen would regularly buy paintings from the annual Royal Academy exhibitions and helped to establish the reputations of artists such as William Powell Frith and Lady Butler. Prince Albert was also

enthusiastic about modern art, even turning his hand to modelling statuettes of his favourite dogs. His personal involvement in coordinating the Great Exhibition of 1851 helped to ensure the success of the project. As their nine children grew up, their marriages strengthened Britain's relationship with other European states: the Princess Royal, also called Victoria, became the wife of the German Kaiser,

5. Music cover: *The Queen and Prince Albert's Polka*, about 1840. Designed by John Brandard. Printed by M. & N. Hanhart. Published by Jullien, London. Colour lithograph. VAM E.828-1959.

6. *The First of May 1851*. By Franz Xavier Winterhalter. The Duke of Wellington presenting a birthday gift to the Prince Arthur on the opening day of the Great Exhibition. Oil on canvas. © The Royal Collection.

8. Queen Victoria in mourning at Windsor, 1863. *Carte de visite* by Bambridge. Albumen print. VAM 3517-1953.

9. *Prince Albert in a kilt*, about 1850. By J. A. Vinter. after K. Macleay. Lithograph. VAM 22182.

Frederick III; and Prince Alfred married the only daughter of Tsar Alexander II of Russia.

The royal family became a role-model for domestic virtue and affection. The Prince Consort led the way in popularizing the German tradition of celebrating Christmas, introducing the Christmas tree to the royal festivities. In 1852 the royal couple bought an estate at Balmoral in the Scottish Highlands and established new fashions for Scottish tartan and holidays hunting on the moors. Albert's death in December 1861 left the Queen devastated. She went into mourning and largely withdrew from political life. During this time she developed an attachment to one of the ghillies from Balmoral, John Brown.

The Prime Minister, Benjamin Disraeli, gradually became a friend and ally and tried to persuade her to return to her duties. It was thanks to him that the Queen was declared Empress of India in 1876. Although she did not personally visit her imperial territories, the Prince of Wales travelled to India as her representative. Both the Prince and Princess of Wales remained popular figures throughout Victoria's reign, despite rumours of his affairs with actresses and professional beauties like Lillie Langtry. The death of his son, the Duke of Clarence, in 1892 was generally mourned.

The celebration of the Queen's Golden Jubilee in 1887 and Diamond Jubilee 10 years later brought her back into public view, re-establishing Victoria as a great figurehead for Britain and its expanding Empire. When she died on the Isle of Wight on 22 January 1901 the nation mourned the end of an era.

7. Scrapbook containing pictures of the Duke of Clarence, Queen Victoria and the Prince and Princess of Wales, about 1880. VAM 60.W.191.

The changes experienced by France, Italy and Germany were especially dramatic, but no European country in the nineteenth century escaped demands for national self-expression and popular involvement in government, often leading to bloody revolutions. Most European monarchies made some attempt, however reluctant, to accommodate these pressures by establishing parliaments and similar representative bodies. But it was the hunger for national self-expression that was to have a particular impact on design and the decorative arts. Across Europe, the embattled advocates of a multitude of nationalisms promoted peasant crafts and folk art as key elements of national identity.

Victorian Britain was not immune to these pressures, although the political power of the British monarch was already very limited at the start of Victoria's reign. Political authority resided principally with the elected Members of Parliament. Yet even after the changes introduced by the Great Reform Act of 1832, Parliament was elected by only a tiny proportion of the British population – a mere 15 per cent of all adult men – among whom the wealthy were heavily over-represented. Despite mass campaigns to secure a democratic constitution, such as those organized by the working-class Chartists in the 1830s and 1840s, it was only very slowly and reluctantly that the governing classes granted the vote to broader sections of the population. The parliamentary Reform Acts of 1867 and 1884 progressively

11

extended the right to vote to men from the more affluent sections of the working classes, but when Victoria died Britain was far from being a democracy. In 1901 two-fifths of adult men were still not eligible to vote, nor were any women. The defining characteristic of the Victorian polity was representative government without democracy.

The emergence of suppressed nationalisms also had its impact on Victorian Britain, most obviously in its relations with Ireland. Before the nineteenth century Great Britain and Ireland had shared a monarch, but had enjoyed separate parliaments. The Act of Union of 1801 finally integrated the two parliaments to form a single United Kingdom of Great Britain and Ireland. Large sections of Irish opinion, especially Irish Catholic opinion, were never reconciled to this arrangement. Campaigns for Irish autonomy were to punctuate Victoria's reign. Towards its end, they became increasingly associated with the efforts of cultural nationalists to construct an ethnically pure Irish identity, unsullied by Anglo-Saxon

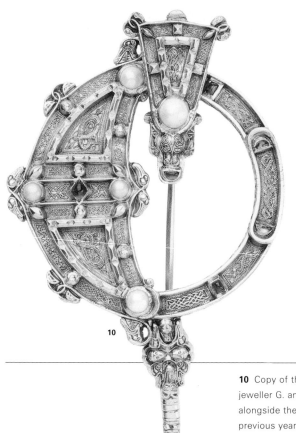

10

10 Copy of the Royal Tara Brooch, about 1851. Made by the Dublin jeweller G. and S. Waterhouse and exhibited at the Great Exhibition, 1851, alongside the early medieval Irish original that had been discovered the previous year near Drogheda, Ireland. Oxidized silver, partially gilded and set with diamonds, amethysts and river pearls. VAM 920-1852.

11 Tartan bag, about 1850. Embroidered silk, trimmed with silk cords and tassels. VAM T.67-1961.

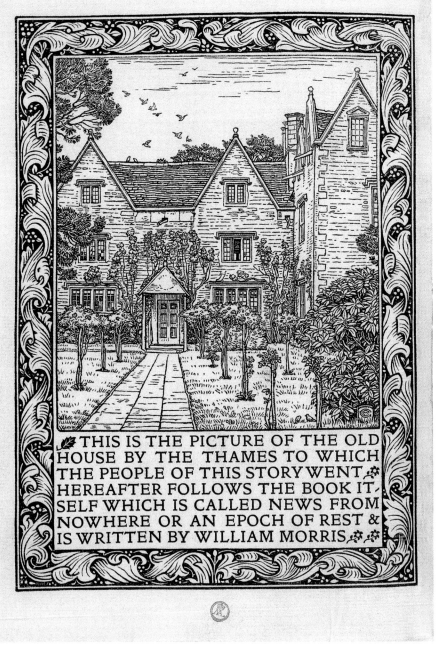

influences. Their efforts focused on the promotion of the Irish language, Gaelic sports and decorative art employing medieval Irish forms and motifs.

In the other territories that comprised the United Kingdom there was little pressure for political separation, but cultural nationalisms flourished within the context of a broader commitment to Britain. As in the rest of nineteenth-century Europe, the search for the essential characteristics of the nation and its people led to those peripheral rural areas that seemed least contaminated by modern commerce. Elements of rural life were selected for imaginative reconstruction into a national culture of questionable authenticity. In Scotland, a rapidly industrializing country, national identity in the Victorian era came to focus on an idealized version of the life and history of the rural Highlands, with particular emphasis on tartan, the kilt and the baronial style of architecture. Victoria and Albert's enthusiasm for their Highland estate at Balmoral gave added respectability to this romanticized version of Scottish identity. In Wales, cultural nationalism was more heavily concentrated on the Welsh language, still widely spoken in rural areas, but an idealized national costume also enjoyed considerable popularity. In England, it was more common for national identity to reside simply in an outward-looking celebration of British commercial and imperial success. Nevertheless, it is possible to detect here, too, a search for the essence of race and nation in a romanticized rural past, especially in the rediscovery of an old English vernacular architecture.

12 A page from a sketchbook depicting girls wearing Welsh hats, 1800–50. By an unknown artist. Pencil on paper. VAM E.3243-1931.

13 Frontispiece from *News from Nowhere* by William Morris, 1892. It depicts Kelmscott Manor, Oxfordshire, the 16th-century English vernacular house that Morris rented in 1871 and described as 'a heaven on earth'. Woodcut. VAM 883-1893.

14

In continental Europe, the rise of nationalism led to warfare, in particular the wars that forged Germany and Italy into nation states during the mid-Victorian years. For most of Victoria's reign, Britain's direct involvement in these and other conflicts on the continent remained diplomatic rather than military. With the exception of the brief Crimean War, fought against Russia between 1854 and 1856, Victorian Britain enjoyed a long peace with its European neighbours. Britain's capacity to remain aloof, though not entirely disengaged, from continental quarrels was most obviously a reflection of the strength of her navy and the weakness of her army. It also reflected a widely held British belief in the country's superiority over her continental neighbours – a superiority that was simultaneously economic, political and moral. Those who governed Victorian Britain did not flinch from competition with her European neighbours, but they preferred the peaceful competition of the international market to military engagements on the battlefield.

14 *The Channel Squadron*, 1898. By Eduardo de Martino. Britain sustained her naval supremacy during the Victorian transition from sail to steam. By the end of the 19th century the Royal Navy's capital ships were steam-powered, armour-plated and relied on the firepower of a relatively small number of heavy guns. Oil on canvas. © National Maritime Museum, London.

15 *Imperial Federation Map of the World*, 1886. From *The Graphic*, 24 July 1886. Colour lithograph. VAM PP.8.D-E.

17

3. Empire

The long Victorian peace did not extend to the wider world beyond Europe. There the process of British imperial expansion by threat and force that had characterized the later Georgian years continued unabated. In an age of rampant imperialism, Victorian Britain was the world's greatest imperial power. By the end of Victoria's reign, it controlled one-quarter of the world's surface and one-fifth of its population. As the leading conservative politician, Benjamin Disraeli, declared in 1866, 'there is no power that interferes more than England. She interferes in Asia, because she is really more an Asiatic Power than a European. She interferes in Australia, in Africa, and New Zealand.' Yet there was no single motive at work behind the seizure of new territories. In some cases, like Hong Kong in 1842, the objective was to open up new markets for British trade. In others, like the annexations in India that followed what the British called the Mutiny of 1857, the aim was to consolidate and safeguard existing territories in the face of local opposition. In yet others, like West Africa, the goal was to forestall the expansion of rival European powers.

The immediate causes of imperial expansion were, therefore, diverse. Nevertheless it would be wrong to ignore the cumulative power of the imperial imperative. The complaints of liberal politicians like William Gladstone, that colonial expansion was often pointless and expensive, did little to stop it, even when the complaints came from politicians who themselves controlled the levers of government. A powerful predisposition towards imperial expansion held sway both in Britain itself and among British officials stationed across the non-European world. It was grounded in a belief in the universal benefits of open trade and Christian (and more especially British) civilization. It drew on the conviction that Britain had a right to safeguard its existing colonial possessions against native peoples and other European powers. It reflected the fact that expansion was relatively painless, given the extraordinary and unprecedented superiority of European military technologies over those available to non-European peoples. It was fuelled by a long-standing belief that the non-white races were intellectually and culturally inferior and might require not just guidance, but also subjection. This belief found renewed vigour after the publication of Charles Darwin's *On the Origin of Species* in 1859, when a vulgarized version of Darwin's theory of the evolution of species was applied to human racial groups, conveniently suggesting that the white races were superior as the result of a process of natural selection. The new, harsher, pseudo-scientific racism played well in the chorus of imperial enthusiasm that dominated the final decades of Victoria's reign.

16

17

16 'Jubilee' wallpaper, 1887. From the stock of F. Scott & Son, 26 High Street, Hawick, Roxburghshire. Colour print from engraved rollers. VAM E.791-1970.

17 Charles Darwin, about 1860. By Julia Margaret Cameron. Albumen print. VAM 14-1939.

THE BRITISH EMPIRE, 1848 AND 1902

John Styles

In 1848, in the early years of Victoria's reign, Britain was already the world's greatest imperial power, controlling more people and territory across the globe than any of its European competitors. The British Empire continued to expand up to the end of the Boer War in 1902, especially in India, Africa and the Pacific, although it was not to achieve its greatest territorial extent until after 1918. Territorial expansion was accompanied by the rationalization of imperial government and, in the later Victorian years, by an increasingly jingoistic celebration of Empire, both in Britain and overseas. Formal control of British India was finally transferred from the East India Company to the British Crown in the aftermath of the Indian Mutiny of 1857; Queen Victoria was declared Empress of India in 1876. Self-government was granted to the colonies of white settlement in Canada, Australia and New Zealand, but elsewhere emerging demands for political representation from native peoples were resisted.

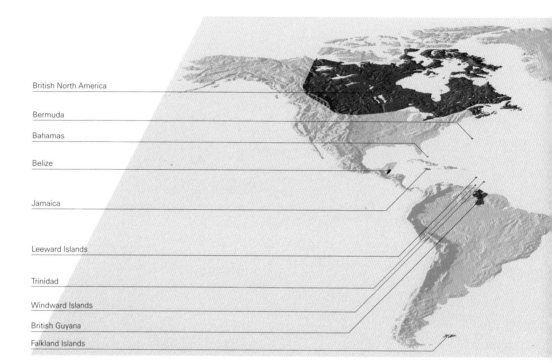

British North America

Bermuda

Bahamas

Belize

Jamaica

Leeward Islands

Trinidad

Windward Islands

British Guyana

Falkland Islands

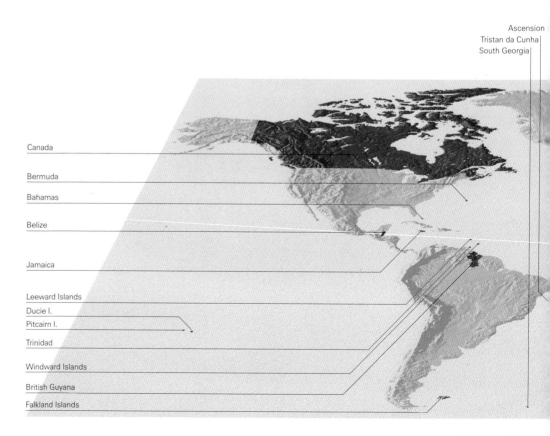

Ascension
Tristan da Cunha
South Georgia

Canada

Bermuda

Bahamas

Belize

Jamaica

Leeward Islands
Ducie I.
Pitcairn I.
Trinidad

Windward Islands

British Guyana
Falkland Islands

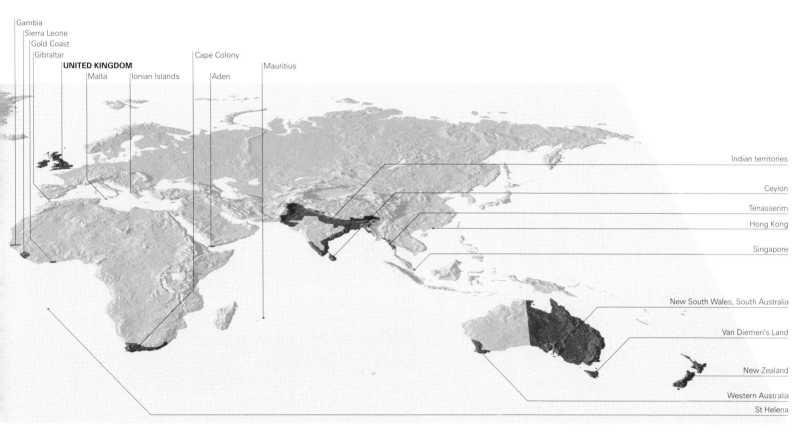

Gambia
Sierra Leone
Gold Coast
Gibraltar
UNITED KINGDOM
Malta   Ionian Islands
Cape Colony
Aden
Mauritius

Indian territories
Ceylon
Tenasserim
Hong Kong
Singapore
New South Wales, South Australia
Van Diemen's Land
New Zealand
Western Australia
St Helena

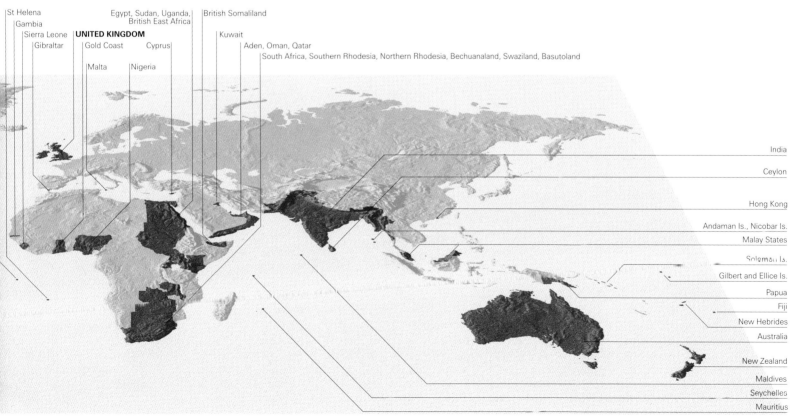

St Helena
Gambia
Sierra Leone   UNITED KINGDOM
Gibraltar   Gold Coast   Cyprus
Malta   Nigeria
Egypt, Sudan, Uganda,
British East Africa
British Somaliland
Kuwait
Aden, Oman, Qatar
South Africa, Southern Rhodesia, Northern Rhodesia, Bechuanaland, Swaziland, Basutoland

India
Ceylon
Hong Kong
Andaman Is., Nicobar Is.
Malay States
Solomon Is.
Gilbert and Ellice Is.
Papua
Fiji
New Hebrides
Australia
New Zealand
Maldives
Seychelles
Mauritius

Nevertheless, it would be wrong to imagine that Victorian attitudes to the peoples and cultures of the non-European world amounted simply to brutal racist disdain. The new biological racism was never as influential in Britain as in many of her European neighbours. Indeed, in design and the decorative arts it is the consistent Victorian enthusiasm for non-European objects that is most striking. Islamic ceramics, Indian textiles and Japanese prints may have been products of what were regarded as less commercially advanced civilizations, but in the eyes of Victorian designers and critics this was precisely what accounted for their aesthetic superiority. In their use of colour, form and decoration these objects surpassed what many regarded as the unprincipled disorder of a European decorative art corrupted by a ceaseless search for mere commercial novelty.

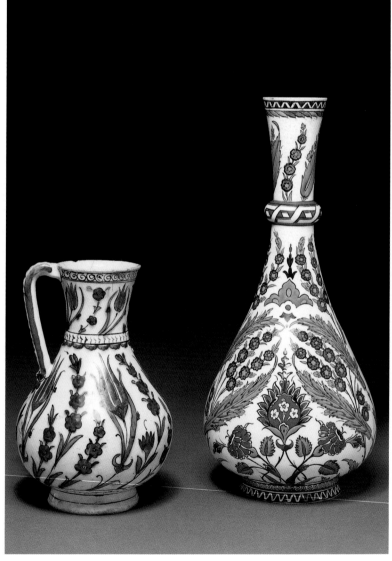

18 Embroidered muslin from Madras, 1868. From *The Textile Fabrics of India* by James Forbes-Watson, vol. VII, 1868. A page from one of the volumes of Indian textile samples assembled by Forbes-Watson, copies of which were supplied to museums and schools of design throughout Britain with the aim of improving British textile design. Cotton muslin with gold embroidery mounted on paper. VAM Indian and South-East Asian Department Library.

19 Left: jug, about 1600. Made at Iznik in Turkey (Anatolia). Siliceous-glazed earthenware, painted. Right: bottle, about 1862. Made by Minton & Co., Stoke-on-Trent. Bone china, painted in underglaze and overglaze colours. Large manufacturers such as Minton & Co. produced ceramics in the fashionable Turkish or Persian (Iranian) style. Shapes, colours and decoration were taken from historical examples, often found in museums and private collections of the 1860s. VAM 728-1893, 8098-1963.

4. Manufacturing

In the 1850s and 1860s Britain made close to half of all the manufactured goods that were traded around the world. It was at one and the same time the world's greatest manufacturing and trading nation. In almost every category of manufactured good and at almost every level of the market the British were perceived by their foreign rivals as immensely effective competitors. With British-made goods so dominant in world trade, British design and decorative arts could hardly fail to have a huge international impact. But British mastery of trade and manufactures was not absolute. Competitors like the French were able to find solace in the superiority of their expensive textiles, furniture and ceramics. The British agonized over the aesthetic shortcomings of their high-

design goods. To assess the role of design and the decorative arts in the workshop of the world, we need to examine the elements that made up the British industrial economy in its Victorian heyday.

The most effective way to do this is to consider Britain's trade in manufactured goods. For most of Victoria's reign, Britain was more reliant on overseas markets for manufactured goods than rivals like France, Germany or the United States, and it exported a greater share of its industrial output. But its main manufactured exports consisted of a very slim range of goods, principally cotton yarn and cloth (much of it plain), and iron and steel in the form of sheets, bars, rails and wire. These were the products of that remarkably narrow, but hugely successful range of industries that were the principal users

---

20 *The Wealth of England: the Bessemer Convertor*, 1895. By W. H. Titcomb. The painting depicts the interior of a steelworks at Rotherham, Yorkshire. The English inventor and industrialist Henry Bessemer developed a process in the 1850s for converting iron into steel by blowing air through molten iron. It was the first of a number of technical innovations that enabled steel to be produced cheaply and in vast quantities. As a consequence, by the end of the 19th century steel had replaced iron in most of its uses. Oil on canvas. Sheffield Industrial Museums Trust Ltd.

21

of steam power. In other words, Britain's decisive advantage over her competitors lay in the products of factory and furnace; in the export of what were often semi-finished goods, produced by the coal-based technologies that the British had developed so successfully during the period 1760–1850. Her advantage was not so decisive when it came to the multitude of finished consumer goods that relied heavily on qualities of visual design and skilled hand labour. In the manufacture of these goods – the products of workshop and sweatshop – steam power was either not used at all (as in the manufacture of glasswares) or only for one or two out of a long sequence of different processes (as in pottery and furniture). As far as goods of this kind were concerned, Britain was often a successful exporter, but not a dominant one. The economist W. S. Jevons noted the implications of this when he compared the economies of Britain and continental Europe in the 1860s. 'Great Britain,' he argued, was 'capable for the present of indefinitely producing all products depending on the use of coal'. Europe, by contrast, was 'capable of an

22

---

21 *Apsley Pellatt's Falcon Glassworks, Southwark, London*, about 1840. By an unknown artist. Oil on canvas. The Museum of London.

22 *The Dinner Hour, Wigan, Lancashire*, 1874. By Eyre Crowe. The painting depicts the mainly female workforce of Wigan's steam-powered cotton mills. Oil on canvas. Manchester City Art Gallery.

23 *Launching a buoy on the Great Eastern*, 1866. By Robert Dudley. Plate from *The Atlantic Telegraph* by W. H. Russell, published in London, 1866. The plate shows a buoy being launched to mark the spot where the Atlantic telegraph cable had been grappled and mended during the third, successful attempt to lay a transatlantic cable. Colour lithograph. Science Museum, London.

indefinite production of artistic, luxurious, or semi-tropical products, but debarred by comparative want of coal from competition with us'.

The limitations of British industrial dominance become clearer still if we examine the destinations of British manufactured exports during the Victorian era. Increasingly these went to the less developed parts of the non-European world, including Britain's own colonies. The proportion of exports that went to the developed economies of Germany and the United States declined, while the proportion that went to the less sophisticated economies of Africa and Asia rose, with India in particular becoming more and more important. This shift was not necessarily to the disadvantage of the British economy as a whole, at least in the short term. It was an element in that broader Victorian process of globalization, facilitated by innovations like the telegraph, the railway, the steam ship and refrigeration, which resulted in ever more complex patterns of economic specialization throughout the world. Asian and African markets were buoyant, growing and profitable. But competition in these markets was less intense. They were less likely than the developed countries to

24 *Modelling*, 1874. From *The Graphic*, 7 November 1874. The modelling room at Elkington and Co. of Birmingham, manufacturers of silver plate. Wood engraving. VAM P.P.8.D.

25 *The Slitting Room for Pens*, 1851. From the *Illustrated London News*, 22 February 1851. Women workers in the factory of Messrs Hinks, Wells and Co. of Birmingham, steel-pen manufacturers, slit pen-nibs using hand-operated machines. Wood engraving. VAM P.P.10.

require goods that were at the international cutting-edge of design and product innovation. Even when they imported goods with a high visual design content, it was a content that was often tailored to very specific local tastes and conditions, like the printed cottons made in Lancashire solely for the Indian market.

It would be wrong to regard this shift towards less sophisticated markets simply as evidence for the shortcomings of British manufacturing. Partly it resulted from the erection of high tariff barriers in the developed world. The international trend to free trade, promoted by the British in the middle years of the nineteenth century, was reversed after 1870. Though Britain remained loyal to free trade, other developed countries became more protectionist in the increasingly nationalist and imperialist climate of the late Victorian years. By the late 1890s, for example, Bradford manufacturers of worsted cloth for men's coats and suits had to pay a customs duty that was greater than the cloth's original value when they exported it to the United States. As a consequence, Americans were obliged to pay more than twice as much as purchasers in

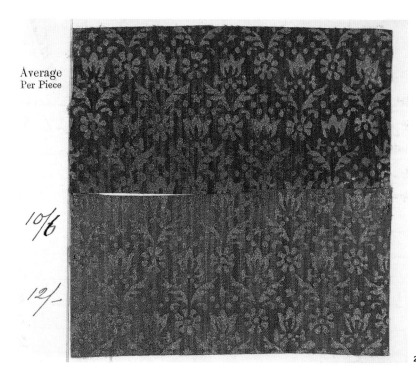

Average Per Piece

10/6

12/-

27

Britain to acquire the same cloth. Exports collapsed. Partly, too, the shift towards less sophisticated markets reflected the vast sums British financiers invested in the less developed countries, both within the Empire and beyond. Much of this investment paid for building railways, harbours and other infrastructure that soaked up the products of British heavy industry.

But it is striking that the shift in British exports to less developed markets in Africa and Asia went hand-in-hand with increasing British imports of manufactured goods from Europe and North America. At the start of Victoria's reign, Britain had imported very few manufactured goods. The growth of manufactured imports suggests that the workshop of the world was becoming increasingly uncompetitive in a number of industries as Victoria grew older. British-made products that suffered at the hands of foreign imports included high-design goods like woven silk fabrics, fine worsted cloth, porcelain and hand-blown wine glasses and decanters. Moreover, this trend was not confined to established industries. Britain also lagged behind her industrialized competitors in a number of the new technologies of the late nineteenth century – electrical goods, dyestuffs, small machines for office and home, such as the typewriter and sewing machine, and, at the very end of the Victorian era, the motor car. Nevertheless, it is important to stress that at no point in Victoria's reign was the overall contribution of British manufacturing to national wealth and trade seriously threatened. Industrial output and industrial exports grew enormously. Still, there was a real economic justification for the anxieties about the quality of British high-design goods that so exercised many Victorians and did so much to promote design education.

26 Poster for the Empire typewriter, 1897. By Lucien Faure. Colour lithograph. VAM Circ.586-1962.

27 Samples of 'goldings', 1888. 'Goldings' were an expensive cotton cloth, printed with a gold pigment, produced in Lancashire for the Indian market. These examples were printed at the Abbey Print Works, Whalley, Lancashire, on 11 October 1888. Printed cotton. Lancashire County Record Office.

5. People

During the reign of Queen Victoria, Britain was the richest country the world had ever known. By the time of her death a progressive increase in national wealth had brought at least some benefits to almost every section of the country's ever-growing population, which doubled from less than 19 million in 1841 to 37 million in 1901. As more and more people came to enjoy increased spending power, the domestic markets for a multiplicity of decorative goods expanded enormously. At the same time, these markets became ever more minutely graded according to wealth and status, with manufacturers producing household goods like clocks and coffee pots to a huge range of specifications, carefully contrived for every taste and pocket. For this remained a profoundly unequal society, one in which even minor distinctions of income, occupation or belief were signalled by the clothes one wore or the way one furnished one's home.

The Victorian era was the first in which it was common to think about society in terms of broad social classes constituted by patterns of work and ownership – the working class, the middle class and the upper class. Few Victorians, at any social level, wholeheartedly embraced the socialists' belief in class exploitation and the inevitability of class conflict. The social distinctions that most concerned them were often ones of status or manners, which did not fit straightforwardly into the grand class categories – distinctions between skilled workers and white-collar clerks with similar incomes, or between the respectable and the rough. Nevertheless, the vocabulary of class distinction was widely employed, albeit with little precision or consistency. Its ubiquity is evidence of the aggressiveness of economic and other inequalities in the Victorian era. The resulting snobberies, anxieties and resentments were very keenly felt.

The summit of the Victorian social pyramid was inhabited by a small but mixed group of astonishingly wealthy families, whose riches derived from land, commerce and manufacturing. The most surprising feature of this élite of wealth, given that Britain had become a predominantly urban nation by the early years of Victoria's reign, was the continuing prominence of rural landowners. The landed aristocracy – as the landed super-rich were increasingly referred to in the nineteenth century – was never precisely defined, but was loosely coterminous with the 4,000 people who in 1873 owned well over half the land in England and Wales, and their Scottish equivalents. These people and their families retained an extraordinarily powerful influence on national politics and London high society. Their significance for design and the decorative arts was immense, most obviously because, before the agricultural depression of the 1870s, many of them went on building and rebuilding vast country houses. These became ever larger and more expensively furnished, incorporating the most up-to-date notions of design, comfort, convenience and sanitation. Remodelling houses like the

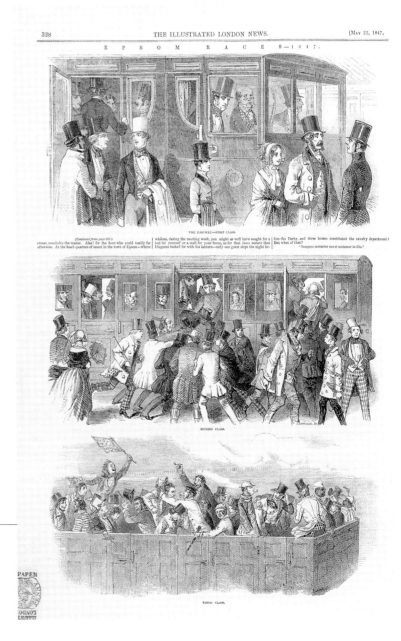

28 A page from *A Catalogue of Christmas, New Year's, Birthday and Wedding Presents*, 1860–70. Published by Silber and Fleming of London, silversmiths. Engraving. VAM TC.C. Box 2.

29 *Epsom Races*, 1847. From the *Illustrated London News*, 22 May 1847. The engravings depict the three classes of railway-excursion passengers on their way to the races at Epsom in Surrey. Wood engraving. VAM P.P.10.

Marquis of Westminster's Eaton Hall in Cheshire, or the Duke of Northumberland's Alnwick Castle, could involve extraordinary expense, in these instances £600,000 and £250,000 respectively. The value of such houses to their owners lay in a combination of social and political functions. They were at one and the same time essential emblems of status and indispensable tools of political hospitality and display.

The fact that the great rural landowners continued to form the largest single segment of the super-rich until the end of the century was testimony to the size of their estates, their ownership of urban and industrial property as well as broad agricultural acres, and their ability to diversify their incomes as agricultural profitability declined. Landed wealth, moreover, was to go on enjoying an exclusive social cachet well into the twentieth century, bolstered by the continuing allure of ancient noble titles, country-house entertaining, rural sports and the aristocratic London season. Yet as Victoria's reign progressed, such wealth was approached, though not matched, by ever-increasing numbers of men with vast fortunes made in the commercial and financial activities concentrated in the City of London. It is ironic, given the prominence of the factory owner as Victorian hero and bogeyman, that for much of Victoria's reign the great non-landed fortunes were generated more readily in banking and trade than in industry. Among those who accumulated their wealth from business, just as among the established landed aristocracy, there were many who spent some of it as enthusiastic patrons of art, architecture and design. Indeed, considerable numbers of the newly wealthy chose to build, or at least acquire, that most expensive of aesthetic playthings, a country house. They included bankers like Baron Meyer Amschel de Rothschild, who built Mentmore in Buckinghamshire, and industrialists like the armaments manufacturer Lord Armstrong, whose house at Cragside in Northumberland was designed by the architect Norman Shaw. It was only a minority of the newly wealthy, however, who went further and translated their profits into really large country estates, especially after the onset of agricultural depression in the 1870s.

Beneath the rarefied summits of the Victorian social hierarchy inhabited by the super-rich, the growth of manufacturing, commerce and towns accelerated the pre-existing shift in the balance of the population away from the countryside towards the urban middle and working classes. The former embraced an extraordinary diversity of occupations, incomes and lifestyles. They ranged from the wealthy cotton masters of the northern mill towns to struggling corner shopkeepers; from sleek London lawyers to impoverished clerks. What they shared was an overlapping set of concerns with the rights of property, the pursuit of respectability, the maintenance of privacy and the avoidance of manual labour — concerns that were hard to pursue without a minimum income of at least £100 a year. By this broad definition, the middle classes comprised about one-fifth of the urban population, a proportion that increased only slowly during Victoria's reign.

30 Mentmore Towers, about 1910. Built 1850–5 to designs by Sir Joseph Paxton and George Henry Stokes for the banker Baron Meyer Amschel de Rothschild. Photographic postcard. Buckinghamshire County Council.

31 Design for the clock tower and chapel at Eaton Hall, Cheshire, 1875. By Alfred Waterhouse for the Duke of Westminster. Pen, ink and watercolour. VAM D.1880-1908.

32

Nevertheless, because the population of the towns grew so fast, the actual number of those in middle-class occupations multiplied, from perhaps a little under a million in 1851 to nearer one and three-quarter million by 1891.

Their households comprised a huge and growing market for decorative goods of all kinds. The least affluent among them enjoyed sufficient spending power to make such purchases, particularly as prices fell with the advent of new manufacturing techniques and materials. Furnishing the home was a particular focus of middle-class investment, both financial and emotional. The middle classes were especially keen to endow the home with moral significance as a sanctuary from the competitive, masculine world of business. Decorating the home was regarded as a distinctively female talent and responsibility. But spending on decorative goods was also a matter of keeping up appearances. Middle-class propriety required the acquisition of those items of clothing and furniture that signalled middle-class status in all its many gradations – carpets, curtains, overmantel mirrors, ornamented furniture, pianos and all manner of fancy goods, from paperweights to wax flowers.

Paradoxically, those who inhabited the various strata of the middle class were expected not simply to own the repertoire of decorative items appropriate to their particular level, but also to display evidence of individual taste and sensibility in their household possessions. Hence the multiplication of ornamental styles, the desperate search for visual novelty and the so-called 'artistic' embellishments that characterized goods made by manufacturers serving this market.

Below the middle class in the social hierarchy, but sometimes overlapping with its lower echelons in income, resided the vast majority of the nation's population – the manual workers and their families who comprised the working class. As with the middle classes, manual workers were divided into overlapping hierarchies, which depended on distinctions such as those between the skilled and unskilled, the respectable and the rough, and the independent and the pauperized. All manual workers, however, shared a vulnerability to the vicissitudes of unemployment and ill health. Even the most prosperous among them spent most of what they earned on housing and food.

32 *An Anxious Hour*, 1865. By Mrs Alexander Farmer. An idealized mother portrayed as the physical and moral nurturer of her family and her home. Oil on panel. VAM 541-1905.

33

Among the utterly impoverished of the urban slums, ragged clothes and bare rooms with a few sticks of broken furniture were common enough. Nevertheless, British workers were, on average, better housed than their German and French equivalents and, from the middle of Victoria's reign, experienced significant improvements in their purchasing power. Even in the poorer working-class households there existed a powerful desire to make a show, to mark out a place in the local pecking order, where status was judged by the ability to possess goods. Walter Besant, the social reformer, described the

33 *A cottage interior*, about 1883. By Alfred Edward Emslie. The walls of this sparsely furnished interior are decorated with framed pictures, cheap prints and fans. Albumen print. VAM E.8822-1994.

two-room tenements of the East End of London at the end of Victoria's reign, where one of the rooms would contain little more than a table, chairs and a chest of drawers:

> On this chest stands a structure of artificial flowers under a glass shade. This is a sacred symbol of respectability . . . On each side of the glass shade are arranged the cups and saucers, plates and drinking glasses, belonging to the family. There are also exhibited with pride all the bottles of medicine recently taken by the various members.

Among workers in skilled or specialist occupations with high earnings, much more impressive forms of display could be achieved. Here, the front room or parlour was the ultimate symbol of respectability, where all the most flamboyant and expensive possessions were located – heavy mahogany furniture, a mirror, patterned linoleum, perhaps even a piano. Middle-class social reformers, like Mrs Samuel Barnett in 1906, disapproved on grounds of both economy and taste:

> In most rooms there is too much furniture and there are too many ornaments . . . I have counted as many as seventeen ornaments on one mantelpiece – three, or perhaps five are ample. She who aims to be thrifty will fight against yielding to the artificially developed instinct to possess.

Yet it is far from clear that the desire to possess such objects needed to be developed artificially. It was a well-entrenched feature of a working-class culture that placed a high value on these and other forms of conspicuous consumption.

6. The urban condition

For all but the very early years of Victoria's reign most British men and women lived in towns; 1851 was the first year in which less than half the British people were recorded as living in the countryside; by 1901 the urban share of the population had grown to three-quarters. Of course, the urban experience was not unfamiliar to the British. At Victoria's accession, London had already been western Europe's largest city for a century and a half. It remained the world's largest city for the whole of the nineteenth century, with approximately a million people at its start and four and a half million at its end. Nevertheless, the fact that for the first time in human history the majority of the inhabitants of a large and populous nation like Britain had ceased to live in the countryside was a momentous one, evoking feelings of both pride and foreboding. Above all, it contributed to the Victorians' acute sense of their own modernity, their sense that humanity's ever-growing power over nature was remaking their world in ways that seemed to have no historical precedent.

34 A Scottish working-class living room, about 1880. The respectable Scottish working-class family depicted in this carefully posed photograph has relatively few domestic possessions, but what it has are carefully arranged and displayed. Hamilton Museum.

35 *Ludgate Hill and St Paul's*, 1887. By William Logsdail. This painting suggests the hectic pace of life in the world's largest city towards the end of the 19th century. Oil on canvas. Private collection.

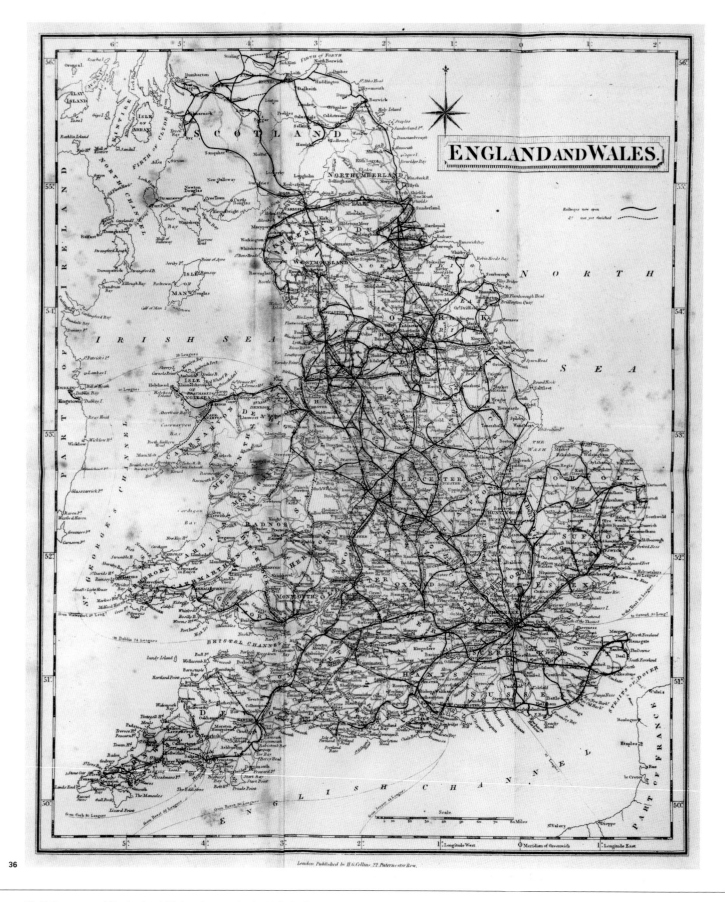

ENGLAND AND WALES.

36 *Railway map of England and Wales*, about 1852. By H. G. Collins.
Much of the national railway network depicted on this map had been laid
out in the course of the previous decade. Engraving. Bodleian Library.

37 *Scene at Ludgate Circus*, 1850. By Eugène
Louis Lami. Omnibuses caught in a London
traffic jam, a characteristically urban
experience. Watercolour. VAM 167-1880.

37

There was no more powerful symbol of this urban modernity than the railway. By 1852 a rudimentary national network was in place connecting the major towns, with well over 6,000 miles (9,650km) of track. It was to go on being extended until the end of the century, when that mileage had nearly trebled. On that network the power of steam moved people and goods at previously unimagined speeds in ways that transformed space and time. As one early observer of the railways commented, 'what was quick is now slow; what was distant is now near'. The railways had the effect of urbanizing the countryside, grinding down local peculiarities with the tools of speed, accessibility and information. They also transformed the appearance of Victorian towns, creating vast new stations and smashing viaducts through

established neighbourhoods, encouraging the growth of suburbs. Moreover, the railway was not the only new form of communication working to collapse many of the distinctions between town and town, and between town and country. The telegraph and later the telephone, the proliferation of inexpensive newspapers and magazines – all contributed to this process. Within the larger towns the omnibus, the tram and the underground railway had similar effects. Victorians felt they were living without a pause. The life of haste, a hurrying pace that was previously associated only with the largest cities, seemed now to be becoming universal.

And of course Victorian urban life could be hellish. Bradford in Yorkshire was one of the fastest-growing factory towns of the early Victorian years. The town was ill prepared to receive the migrants who flocked there, looking for work in its mills, mines and quarries. Houses, roads, sewers and other facilities were grossly inadequate. The consequences for many of the town's poorer inhabitants were overcrowding, pollution and ill health. Average life expectancy in the town during the 1840s was barely 20 years; the rate of infant mortality was the fifth-highest in the country; a cholera epidemic killed 426 people in 1849. Yet in Bradford, as in most other towns, the Victorian years saw a massive – albeit sometimes reluctant – response to the problems and opportunities thrown up by urban growth.

38 *South-east view of Bradford*, 1841. Drawn by Charles Cousen, engraved by J. Cousen. Frontispiece from *The History and Topography of Bradford* by John James, 1841. Smoke from a forest of factory chimneys hangs over one of the fastest-growing industrial towns of the 1840s. Engraving. VAM 258.e.

Most important in its implications for design and the decorative arts was the creation of a whole range of new urban institutions, undertaken both by municipal and private enterprise. National and local government built town halls, market halls, libraries, art galleries, schools, prisons, asylums and sanitary facilities. All of these had to be designed and most of them furnished; so too did the 20,000 new churches built in Victoria's reign to minister to the spiritual needs of the new town dwellers, and the theatres and music halls, the pubs and clubs that provided more mundane forms of entertainment. The new railways required stations and hotels to accommodate the increasing number of travellers. Factories, warehouses and banks all had to be designed and fitted out, as did the department stores and other grand retail outlets that added a new scale and splendour to the experience of shopping.

What we are observing here is the growth of corporate design patronage, which flowed from both the public and private sectors. The size of the new corporate organizations could be immense. The North Eastern Railway alone employed 33,000 people in 1884, as many as the peacetime army in the mid-eighteenth century. Architects were no longer confined mainly to designing churches and country houses, as they had been for centuries. They thus tended to become more specialized, while acquiring the trappings of a profession. Corporate commissions also provided a constant flow of new work for suppliers of furnishings and fittings, some of them on an extremely large scale. Morris and Company, which supplied stained glass for churches, and Minton and Company, which supplied tiles for the new Palace of Westminster, are two famous examples out of thousands of firms that benefited.

The important role played by the state (national and local) as a patron of architecture and design seems superficially at odds with the widely held Victorian view that government should be non-interventionist in its policies and frugal in its expenditure. Yet Victorian governments were rarely consistent in applying the doctrine of 'laissez-faire', however much they might pay lip service to it. This was particularly true in the field of design. Government-subsidized schools of design began to be set up from 1837, and by 1849 there were already 21. Government encouraged the Great Exhibition, although it did not pay for it. Subsequently it did fund the South Kensington Museum (later the Victoria and Albert Museum) as an adjunct to the Government School of Design. The cumulative outcome of these initiatives was that mid-Victorian Britain enjoyed a national, government-funded system of design education at least as extensive as that of a number of its competitors.

39 *The London Bridge Terminus Coffee Room*, about 1862. By Robert Dudley. Colour lithograph. The Museum of London.

40 *Bradford town hall*, 1872. Bradford's neo-Gothic town hall was completed in 1872 to a design by Messrs Lockwood and Mawson of Bradford, architects. From *The Builder*, 16 November 1872. Wood engraving. VAM P.P.19.G.

41 Tiles, about 1850. Designed by A. W. N. Pugin for the floor at the Palace of Westminster. Made by Minton & Co., Stoke-on-Trent, Staffordshire. Encaustic tiles. VAM C.1-1985.

42 *F. and C. Osler's Oxford Street showroom*, about 1860. Probably painted by Owen Jones. After acquiring their own glassworks in Birmingham, the firm of F. and C. Osler further expanded by building a spectacular showroom in Oxford Street, London, in 1858–60, to a design by Owen Jones. Pen, ink and watercolour on paper. VAM P.29-1976.

42

Moreover, the influence of the Victorian state on design extended beyond direct patronage and education. It also influenced design indirectly through its efforts to promote business competition and restrict monopolies. Thus a legal decision in 1876 prevented the railway companies' own workshops from building locomotives for sale to other customers, a move that tended to reinforce the distinctiveness of each company's locomotive design and the multiplication of designs in use across the national railway network. On a wider scale, the Trades Marks Act of 1875 made it much easier to defend brand names and logos against piracy. This facilitated the late-Victorian proliferation of branded products, with all their accompanying graphic imagery, which led the Tory politician, Lord Randolph Churchill, to assert that 'we live in an age of advertisement, the age of Holloway's pills, of Colman's mustard, and of Horniman's tea'.

7. Ideas

The Victorians debated design and the decorative arts with an extraordinary vigour. Most of these debates turned on the question of what was the appropriate aesthetic response to Victorian modernity in all its manifestations. For many of the participants in these debates this was essentially a moral question. This is not to suggest that the debaters ignored the new scientific discoveries of the age, from the findings of geologists and biologists to the increasingly precise historical understanding of past styles. Nor is it to say that their concerns were exclusively religious. Victorians were steeped in religion. In the aftermath of the evangelical revival of the early nineteenth century, active religious observance was widespread. A high religious seriousness permeated all aspects of public life, while the rivalry between the state church – the Church of England – and its numerous and powerful nonconformist competitors was fundamental to party-political divisions. Nevertheless, Victorian debates over design and aesthetics were not couched in solely religious terms. Fundamentally, the question of what was the appropriate aesthetic response to Victorian modernity was a moral question because it required a moral judgement on the world the Victorians had created. On this issue, many of the leading voices in these debates took a pessimistic view. The tone was set by the architect and designer A. W. N. Pugin in the early Victorian years.

Pugin was not the first to argue that design could be aesthetically good only if it were the product of a good society, but he believed it. He condemned the commercial society of the first half of the nineteenth century as materialistic in its values, unchristian in its philosophy and soulless in its inhumanity towards the poor. He dismissed its dominant style – neo-classicism – in the same terms. A convert from the Anglican Church to Roman Catholicism, he argued that the Gothic was the only moral style because it dated from the medieval period, before the Reformation and before the rise of commerce and capitalism.

43 Henry Cole, 1870. By A. J. Melhuish.
Photograph. VAM 355-1886.

44 *Advertising hoarding in Bolton*, 1898.
By Alec Davis. The packed hoarding displays posters for a huge variety of branded products. VAM Prints, Drawings and Paintings Department Library.

Gothic was the style of a society that, according to Pugin's interpretation of the Middle Ages, was Christian, hierarchical and paternalist. In such a society everyone knew their place, but also knew their duty, in particular the solemn religious duty of the wealthy to help the poor. But for Pugin design was a moral issue in another, slightly different sense. He believed the aesthetic quality of design to be linked to honesty of construction. He insisted that the construction of an object should be honestly displayed, not concealed beneath illusionistic and hence deceitful decoration. Good artefacts were those that visibly avoided any taint of deception.

Pugin died in 1852, but his views were subsequently to be taken up by many who were neither Catholics nor pessimists about the modern condition.

Indeed, it was possible for elements of Pugin's ideas to appeal to both sides of the profound rift in Victorian thinking, which divided those who believed in the capacity of rationality, science and reform to improve the world from those, like Pugin himself, who were critical of modernity, science and economics from a romantic standpoint. Henry Cole, the civil servant who was the leading light behind the Great Exhibition and later head of the government department that ran the schools of design and the South Kensington Museum in London, was a fairly conventional Anglican of a rational, reforming temper. Yet he was to become one of the most ardent promoters of Pugin's views about honesty of construction and the deceitful nature of illusionistic ornament.

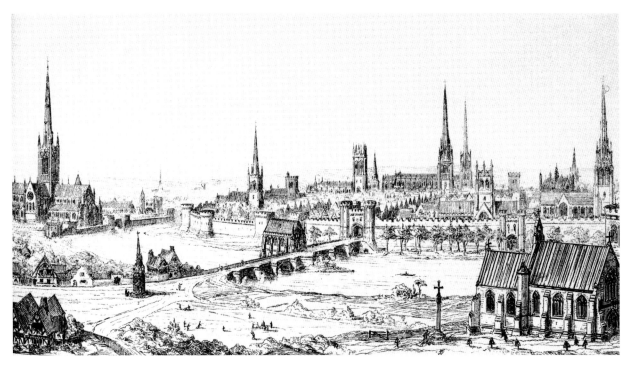

45 *The medieval town and the modern town*, 1836. Plates from *Contrasts; or, A parallel between the noble edifices of the fourteenth and fifteenth centuries and similar buildings of the present day. Shewing the present decay of taste*, by A. W. N. Pugin, 1836. Engraving. VAM Loan: Clive Wainwright.

45

Morris followed Ruskin's advice to 'get rid of any idea of decorative art being a degraded or separate kind of art. Its nature and essence is simply its being fitted for a definite place; and, in that place, forming part of a great and harmonious whole, in companionship with other art.'

Of course, the opinions of Pugin, Cole, Ruskin and Morris do not capture the whole range of the Victorian debate about the visual arts and the modern condition. Nevertheless, they do indicate how important design and the decorative arts were to that debate. They also illustrate its characteristically Victorian tone – above all, its intense moral earnestness. The fundamental moral imperative that these men shared with other Victorian thinkers was a sense of an overwhelming personal duty to act for the common good. The passion they expended in arguing about design reflects a typical Victorian conviction that the exercise of the will for altruistic purposes was essential to an individual's moral health. Acting for the common good was as much about avoiding personal moral stagnation as it was about helping others. Both were fundamental to the key Victorian notion of 'character'. It was only in the 1890s that this moral imperative – what the author Oscar Wilde called 'the sickly cant about Duty' and that 'sordid necessity of living for others' – began to be criticized as priggish and hypocritical. Yet it was not until the 1920s and 1930s that Victorian moral earnestness, like Victorian ornament, came to be widely dismissed as thoroughly out-of-date.

John Ruskin, the greatest cultural critic of the age, was an evangelical Anglican who lost his faith. Centrally concerned with the relationship between aesthetics and nature, to an extent that Pugin was not, he shared Pugin's belief in the degeneracy of modern civilization and in the moral and aesthetic superiority of the Gothic style. Ruskin's greatest disciple was William Morris, the socialist advocate of arts and crafts. Morris, like Ruskin, believed himself to live in a society where ugly, degraded objects were made by tormented workers who found no satisfaction in their work. In Morris's view, objects should be a source of beauty and pleasure for those who made them, as well as for those who used them. This would be possible only if workers were free to exercise their creativity, which they could not under the capitalist division of labour. Only if labour were ennobled, as Morris believed it had been during the Middle Ages, could all objects be beautiful. Art would then become a universal activity in which everybody participated, both as makers and users. This belief that art should include the whole range of everyday artefacts was the key to Morris's passion for the decorative arts. Conventionally they were regarded as inferior to the fine arts of painting and sculpture, but

46 *John Ruskin at the Waterfall*, 1853–4. By John Everett Millais. Oil on canvas. © Tate, London, 2003.

47 Decanter and stopper, with London hallmarks for 1904–5. Designed by C. R. Ashbee; mark of the Guild of Handicraft Limited, Chipping Campden, Gloucestershire; glass probably made by Powell of Whitefriars, London. Ashbee designed several versions of this decanter. Green glass with silver mounts and a chrysoprase set in the finial. VAM M.121-1966.

48 'St George' cabinet, 1861–2. Designed by Philip Webb; made by Morris, Marshall, Faulkner & Co., London; painted by William Morris. The painted scenes are from the legend of St George and the Dragon. The theme epitomizes Morris's youthful enthusiasm for medieval romance and literature. Painted and gilded mahogany, pine and oak, with copper mounts. VAM 341-1906.

8. Towards the twentieth century

The end of Victoria's reign marked a high point in Britain's aesthetic influence. At home there may have been some unease about the rate at which other countries were catching up economically, as well as a new scepticism about conventional morality. Nevertheless, British design enjoyed unprecedented international repute. Only Paris matched London as a focus of international cultural attention.

In design and the decorative arts, British practitioners and ideas were universally esteemed. British high-design objects could be found in homes and palaces, shops and museums across the inhabited world. Even among the avant-garde in continental Europe and America, British designers were key sources of inspiration. This was especially true of those working within the Arts and Crafts idiom, like C. R. Ashbee, whose work was displayed to great acclaim at the Vienna Secession's eighth exhibition in 1900.

Yet British influence was not destined to last. In the twentieth century international leadership in design was to reside elsewhere: in France, Germany and eventually the United States. As the century proceeded, it was the advocates of Modernism, in all its many manifestations in design, architecture and art, who were increasingly to hold sway. Modernism, with its contempt for Victorian ornament and its celebration of machine-made, standardized goods, was a development that Britain, of all the major world powers, was to have the greatest difficulty in accommodating.

49 Desk, 1896. Designed by C. F. A. Voysey as part of a suite of furniture for a house in Bayswater, London. Voysey was one of the most innovative Arts and Crafts designers. This writing desk shows a number of his favourite features. Simple in appearance, the decoration is confined to practical details such as the applied copper hinges. Oak with brass panel and copper hinges. VAM W.6-1953.

CHAPTER 2

Style

MICHAEL SNODIN

1. The great style debate

In 1840 the decorators Henry and Aaron Arrowsmith calmly observed in *The House Decorator and Painter's Guide* that 'the present age is distinguished from all others in having no style which can properly be called its own'. They went on to set out a tempting menu of historical and exotic possibilities, including 'Greek, Roman, Arabesque, Pompeian, Gothic, Cinque Cento, François Premier, and the more modern French'. For other people the lack of a style unique to the age was the most visible sign of a need for design reform. Ornament, they felt, had simply got out of control, and a return to basic principles was needed. The next 60 years were to be marked by a search, by government, critics, architects, artists and designers, to come up not only with a single style appropriate to the modern world but the means to achieve it. The solutions ranged from a government educational programme, based on the study of historical ornament, to the all-encompassing ideas of the Arts and Crafts movement in the 1880s, in which style was incorporated into a complete attitude towards designing and making.

In the end, this reforming drive did nothing to reduce the number of styles on offer. In fact its diverse approaches contributed to making the Victorian period the most stylistically eclectic episode in British history, a veritable bazaar of style, aided by ever-increasing access to cheap, mechanically produced goods. The Victorian treatment of style depended on the idea of synthesis, in which elements from different sources were combined into a new and coherent whole, eventually losing any link with their stylistic parents. The synthetic styles thus produced reflected a hitherto unparalleled knowledge of historical and non-European ornament and design, a fundamentally romantic approach to history and ornament, and a fascination with complexity and intricacy. Significantly, the Victorians' own style names were usually more atmospheric than accurately descriptive. It is hard for us

2

now to distinguish between two very similar neo-rococo chairs of 1851, called respectively Louis XIV and Louis XV. Similarly, the 'Queen Anne' style of the 1870s and 1880s was a charming hotchpotch of various English vernacular ideas taken from the sixteenth to the eighteenth centuries, sharpened by a dash of Japan.

The great Victorian style debate is exemplified by two books and an exhibition. A. W. N. Pugin's *Contrasts; or a Parallel between the noble edifices of the fourteenth and fifteenth centuries and similar buildings of the present day*, published in 1836, was the first work to attach strongly moral, religious and social values to a specific style (*see 3:40*). Pugin was not simply promoting the ideas and values

---

1 Detail of *Design for the interior of Breidenbach's shop, New Bond Street, London*, 1853. By Robert Lewis Roumieu. Breidenbach's, perfumier and distiller of eau-de-cologne to Queen Victoria, was fitted out in a synthesis of French rococo and Italian baroque elements. Pen, ink and watercolour. RIBA Library Drawings Collection.

2 *A design for the side of a room in the Louis Quatorze style*. Plate from *The House Decorator and Painter's Guide* by Henry and Aaron Arrowsmith, 1840. Hand-coloured etching and aquatint. VAM 47.N.34.

of the Middle Ages as a model for the nineteenth century, but was also saying that its style – medieval Gothic correctly treated – was the only true (and Christian) style. Gothic never shook off this moral load, and similar readings were soon being attached to other styles, especially those that opposed it.

Owen Jones's *The Grammar of Ornament*, published in 1856, marked an equally profound shift in the way that styles were perceived, but one that was directly opposed to the moral strain of Pugin. Promoted by the government's design education establishment, the *Grammar*, with its 100 coloured plates categorized by period and style, for the first time presented ornament (and therefore style) as a universal formal language, capable of being analysed and scientifically applied. Jones went on to set out a number of general principles of design and application of ornament, for his aim was not to promote historical revivals but to show how artists should, 'by an attentive examination of the principles which pervade all works of the past, and which have excited universal admiration, be led to the creation of new forms equally beautiful'. Although some of the principles were derived from Pugin, they were wholly free of Pugin's moral drive, except in so far as Jones saw all admiration of natural form as praise of the Creator.

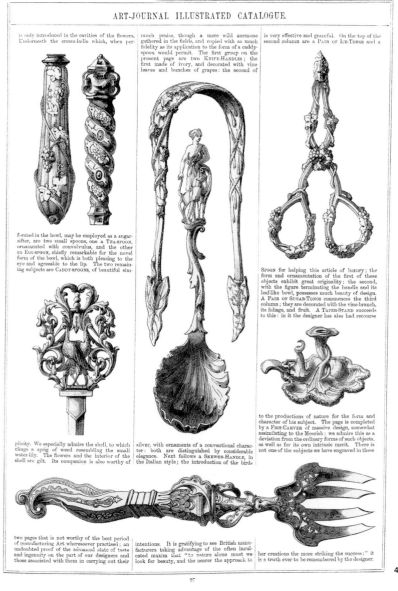

3 *Celtic No. 2*. Plate from *The Grammar of Ornament* by Owen Jones, 1856. Coloured lithograph. VAM L.1625-1986.

4 A page from the *Official descriptive and illustrated catalogue of the Great Exhibition*, 1851. 'There is not one of the subjects we have engraved in these two pages that is not worthy of the best period of manufacturing Art wheresoever practised.' VAM PP. 6.B.

The third key event was the Great Exhibition of 1851. Today, its contents are often held to exemplify the sheer confusion of Victorian design. The art manufactures on display are unfavourably compared with the great iron and glass structure of the Crystal Palace itself, a logical piece of engineering in a which historical style seems to have had no place. Contemporary reactions were very similar, at least among design-reforming critics like Ralph Nicholson Wornum. His essay on the 'The Exhibition as a lesson in Taste' regretted the departure from the Greek and Roman 'taste so active fifty years ago' and the 'endless specimens of the prevailing gorgeous taste of the present day, which gives the eye no resting-place, and presents no idea to the mind, from the want of individuality in its gorged designs'. As a lecturer in the Government School of Design, set up in 1837, Wornum was expressing a particular design-reform agenda which echoed that of the official drive to improve national design. This stemmed originally from a Parliamentary Select Committee, which reported in 1836 that British manufactures were losing the export race, principally because of the low quality of their design. The Exhibition showed that it was not simply a matter of exports but of the reform of national taste itself.

6

2. From Regency to Victorian: classical style

By 1837 almost all the historical styles that were to dominate Victoria's reign were already in use. The classical style, known as 'Greek', was dominant in public interiors and public architecture. Increasingly linear and abstract, it was attacked by Pugin in 1836 as the 'New Square style'. Its days were indeed numbered, at any rate for external architecture; in 1833 the critic and gardener John Claudius Loudon had pointed out that the Greek style, while acceptable in town, was unsuitable for country houses, spelling the beginning of the end for the neo-Palladian tradition in British architecture that had begun with Inigo Jones some 200 years earlier. More prophetic was a lusher style that intermixed classical with baroque and rococo elements, which had emerged in interiors of the 1820s. It was matched at a more modest level by a type of sinuously modelled, simplified classicism, which was characteristic of much furniture of the 1830s and 1840s, often accompanied by violently patterned and brightly coloured wallpaper and furnishing textiles. The second classical strain in architecture was the Italianate, a style derived equally from Picturesque villas and Renaissance *palazzi*. At first applied to large country houses and later to the royal residence of Osborne House (partly designed by Prince Albert), it became, from the 1850s up to the 1870s, the standard style for middle-class houses.

5

---

5 Osborne House, Isle of Wight, built 1845–8. Designed by Prince Albert and Thomas Cubitt.

6 *The Grand Hall and Staircase at Stafford House, London*, about 1843. By Joseph Nash. Stafford House (now called Lancaster House) was begun in 1820 as York House. Benjamin Dean Wyatt completed it from 1827 for the second Marquess of Stafford and his son, the second Duke of Sutherland. The hall and staircase were created in 1825–9 in a classical style with baroque and rococo elements. Watercolour. The Museum of London.

While neo-Palladianism died out in external architecture, in certain circles classical styles continued in favour after 1850, in interiors and household objects, and, reacting to new waves of archaeological discoveries and publications, even took on a greater accuracy. The 'Pompeian' decoration style of the 1860s onwards was matched by accurate (and usable) reproductions of ancient jewellery and furniture. From the 1860s the neo-classical and Empire styles were gradually rediscovered, first of all in exhibition pieces and then less expensively. From the 1870s the interiors of people of 'artistic' taste began to fill up with small, light 'Sheraton' and 'Hepplewhite' furniture (real or reproduction). In the 1890s Adam-style drawing rooms became the fashionable norm.

3. From Regency to Victorian: rococo and naturalism

The mid-eighteenth-century rococo style was first revived in the second decade of the nineteenth century. By the 1820s it was being incorporated into classical interiors. The style was to some extent derived from the English rococo style – notably that of Thomas Chippendale, whose furniture pattern book (as well as those of other English rococo furniture makers and carvers) was being reprinted and reproduced from the 1830s onwards – but was chiefly identified with France and was, indeed, the 'more modern French' style described by the Arrowsmiths. At first presented as a mixed style with the baroque (perhaps accounting for its popular name of 'Louis XIV'), it became in the 1840s a distinctly Louis XV style. In both Britain and France rococo was now the leading style for mainstream luxury decoration, a position that it retains to this day. While it was often used fairly accurately, imaginative variations were emerging by the 1830s, enabling rococo to become the main vehicle for the extravagantly modelled upholstery of the mid-nineteenth century, as well as the origin of the 'balloon back', the most common form of Victorian light chair.

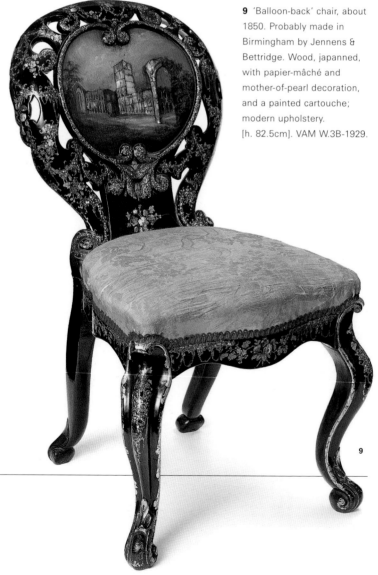

9 'Balloon-back' chair, about 1850. Probably made in Birmingham by Jennens & Bettridge. Wood, japanned, with papier-mâché and mother-of-pearl decoration, and a painted cartouche; modern upholstery. [h. 82.5cm]. VAM W.3B-1929.

7 The drawing room, 118 Mount Street, London, 1894. Carried out in the 'Adam' style by the decorator Howard Hanks, for a Miss Walford. Photograph by H. Bedford Lemere. Albumen print. VAM 230-1926.

8 Coffee pot, with Sheffield hallmarks for 1872–3. Mark of W. & G. Sissons. The engraved horsemen were taken from the Parthenon marbles. Silver. VAM Circ.98-1961.

10

11

4. A break with the past

Naturalism was taken up by Henry Cole, the design reformer and later the first Director of the South Kensington Museum, in his designing and making enterprise, called Felix Summerly's Art Manufactures, which began in 1847. Unlike most other expressions of the naturalistic style, the Summerly objects sought to use natural ornament in a manner appropriate to their function. Thus the 'well-spring' water carafe was decorated with a flower band and abstracted water-reed decoration (complete with decoratively disposed roots at the base), while a christening mug was decorated with protective angels.

The Summerly objects were also designed to combine ornament with practicality. The mug was carefully provided with a wide, undecorated lip for drinking, while a papier-mâché wine tray, unlike other products in the same material, had two practical depressions for glassware. The simplicity and logic of these objects becomes apparent when they are compared with expressions of naturalism shown at the 1851 Exhibition, which, although very popular, horrified design commentators with their stylistic freedom and lack of appropriateness. The artist Richard Redgrave, who had designed the 'well-spring' carafe, turned his back on naturalism in his comments on the Exhibition and, like Ralph Wornum, advocated a return to Renaissance styles and design principles.

The plants and other natural forms that were a traditional part of the rococo style played a leading role in the development of naturalism, which became the most characteristic stylistic expression of the middle years of the century. The naturalistic style involved the use of sculptural figures and organic naturalistic ornament, often with a symbolic – or at least story-telling – intent. This trend, which had begun in the early years of the century, reached its peak in the 1840s and 1850s, with silver, ceramics and other materials being treated in a highly sculptural way. At its least extreme, naturalistic elements were added to objects of traditional form, while at its most developed, figures and organic forms created the whole shape of the object. This was something completely new, creating artefacts that broke entirely with historical exemplars.

12

---

10 *View of a Drawing Room in a London town house*, about 1855. By Samuel Rayner. Decorated in the revived rococo style. Watercolour. VAM E.1167-1948.

11 Gas jet lamp in the form of a convolvulus, the design registered in 1848. Made by the firm of R. W. Winfield, Birmingham. This lamp was shown in the Great Exhibition in 1851 and formed part of Henry Cole's display, in 1852, of Examples of False Principles in Decoration. Gilt brass and glass. VAM M.20-1974.

12 'Wellspring' water carafe, 1847–50. Designed by Richard Redgrave and made by J. F. Christy, Stangate Glassworks, Lambeth, London, for Felix Summerly's Art Manufactures. Glass, painted in enamel. VAM 4503-1901.

5. Plants and ornament: Owen Jones and Christopher Dresser

The official disapproval of naturalism did not extend to the use of natural ornament as a whole. The general enthusiasm for plants (so copiously evident in the naturalistic style) was matched by advances in the scientific categorization of nature and a corresponding drive towards a type of botanical ornament that was based on the scientific study of natural forms. Examples like Redgrave's design exercise on the sow-thistle led to a type of botanical ornament that was both highly decorative and sympathetic to the actual behaviour of plants. This reached its most effective form in the work of William Morris and the Arts and Crafts movement. Owen Jones attempted something more profound, maintaining in *The Grammar of Ornament* that nature had a key role to play in creating a new style that was to be separated from architecturally based historicism. If a student were to 'examine for himself the works of the past, compare them with the works of nature, bend his mind to a thorough appreciation of the principles which reign in each, he cannot fail to be himself a creator, and to individualize new forms, instead of reproducing the forms of the past'. It was left to Jones's disciple, the radical designer Christopher Dresser, to carry his hints into practice during the 1860s.

Today Christopher Dresser is perhaps best known for his designs for startlingly functional ceramics and metalwork of the 1870s and 1880s, which sprang from his central idea of fitness or 'adaptation to purpose'. Dresser's notion that it was possible to produce an 'artistic' object entirely without ornament was certainly revolutionary, but his ideas on ornament, based on botany, were equally daring. Both an art and design theorist and a scientific botanist, Dresser had drawn the plates of natural specimens at the end of Jones's *Grammar* and had lectured at the Government School of Design on artistic botany – that is, the application of scientific botany to design, a subject that he himself had invented. Dresser also preached that ornamentation was a fine art, which should 'ennoble and elevate our fellow-creatures'. Certain treatments of form and colour could, for instance, suggest repose, excitement or melancholy. He also believed that there were certain design principles common to all cultures, leading to a list of 'Grades in the Decorative Arts', from natural adaptations (the lowest form of ornament), through 'conventional treatment of natural form' and mental ideas suggested by nature, to the pinnacle of 'purely ideal ornament' – 'utterly an embodiment of mind in

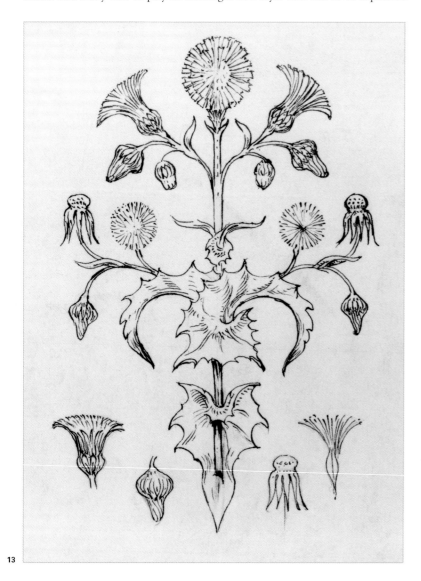

13

13 *A Study of a Sonchus or Sow Thistle*. By Richard Redgrave. Used as an illustration in his *Manual of Design*, 1876: 'the plant is displayed and flattened, whilst the form of the buds, the seed vessels and the leaves, are examined as new motives for ornaments'. Pen and ink. VAM 8452.B.

14

form'. From historical and exotic styles he assigned to the highest grade the 'Greek, the Moorish, the Early English, much of the Indian, and many features of the Japanese, and some parts of Egyptian and Renaissance', while in the lowest lay 'our modern floral patterns'. Perhaps the most extraordinary example of his theory was a pattern used on a Wedgwood vase in 1867, in which, he wrote:

> I have sought to embody chiefly the idea of power, energy, force, or vigour; and in order to do this, I have employed such lines as we see in the bursting buds of spring . . . and especially such as are to seen in the spring growth of a luxuriant tropical vegetation: I have also availed myself of those forms to be seen in certain bones of birds which are associated with the organs of flight . . . as well as those observable in the propelling fins of certain species of fish.

6. Owen Jones and the Near East

The original source of Jones's ideas and analysis of ornament was a close study of Islamic architecture and ornament. Islamic ornament in particular suited his reforming notions, as it was both naturalistic and carried out on geometrical principles. Jones's studies culminated in 1842–5 in the publication of the first serious account of Islamic design, *Plans, Elevations, sections and details of the Alhambra*, a study of the famous Moorish palace in Granada, Spain. The book used lavish chromolithographed plates to illustrate the all-important colouring of the palace interiors. The Islamic use of colour lay at the heart of the colour theories in design that Jones was developing. They were matched by contemporary advances in scientific colour theory, as well as by a growth of interest in the use of colour in ancient Greek and Roman architecture. Jones's colour theories were put into practice most famously at the 1851 Exhibition, where he painted the huge ironwork structure a mixture of primary colours calculated to merge into white at a distance.

Jones's publications led to the adoption of Moorish interlaced patterns and other motifs in textiles, tiles and other fields. At a more general level, the Moorish style was adopted for appropriate interiors,

14 Vase, 1867. Designed by Christopher Dresser. Made by Josiah Wedgwood and Sons, Etruria, Staffordshire, 1867. Earthenware, transfer printed, painted in enamels. John S.M. Scott, Esq.

15 *Window in the Mirador of Lindaraja, The Alhambra, Granada, Spain*. Plate from *Plans, elevations, sections and details of the Alhambra* by Owen Jones and Jules Goury, 1842–5. Coloured lithograph. VAM 110.P.36.

16 Teapot, with London hallmarks for 1850–1. Made for the Great Exhibition by Joseph Angell. The outline form and feet are rococo in style, but the modelling and other decoration are Near Eastern. Silver, parcel-gilt, with enamel decoration and ivory. VAM M.27-1983.

such as smoking rooms, while carefully selected Moorish and Near Eastern furniture and artefacts became an essential part of the art interior in the 1880s and 1890s. This use of exotic styles, which also included Indian and Japanese elements, was very different from the essentially frivolous and fantastic use of exoticism before 1850. By the final decades of the century their context was that of expanding European empires and their sources were the national displays in international exhibitions. But reactions to these exotic artefacts was far from negative, at least among design reformers. The products of India and Japan were perceived as being closer to their design ideal than anything produced at home. In 1852 the Museum of Manufactures, in buying from the Great Exhibition, spent as much on objects from India as from Europe. At the 1862 exhibition the architect William Burges admired the Japanese display as the 'true medieval court' for its attitudes to craft and design.

18

17

7. Gothic style

If any particular style is linked to the Victorian period today it is probably the Gothic Revival. Why should this be? The answer probably lies in the Church, for Gothic was the principal expression of an extraordinarily fervent religious revival. This not only encompassed new churches and their furnishings, but also the more or less vigorous restoration, re-ordering and refurnishing of almost every ancient church in the country in what was seen as the medieval manner. In the domestic architectural field, Gothic was much less in evidence, although it had never fallen out of favour as a suitable style for country houses since its inception in that field in about 1800. By the 1870s mass-produced Gothic details were creeping into ordinary houses. In public and civic buildings, however, Gothic was the leading serious style from the 1850s to the 1870s, although it was in contention with both the classical and the Renaissance styles.

The key event in the establishment of Gothic was the decision, following a disastrous fire in 1834, that the New Palace of Westminster (or Houses of Parliament) should be built in the Gothic or Elizabethan style. The choice was an official recognition that these styles represented the truest expression of British history and national identity. This idea had been growing since the beginning of the century, in tandem with an intensely Romantic attitude to the Middle Ages and the sixteenth century as periods of national glory and social stability. It reached its peak with such events as the Eglinton Tournament of 1839, an attempt by the nobility to re-create a medieval tournament. The same period saw the publication of Tennyson's Arthurian poems and a complete edition of Joseph Nash's *Mansions of England in the Olden Time*, in which the notion of Merry England – with contented peasantry and a benevolent aristocracy – was transplanted into surviving country-house interiors. Nash's imaginary Jacobean and Elizabethan world was backed up by real modern architecture, interiors, furniture and furnishings in the same styles.

17 The Victoria Tower, the Palace of Westminster, London, 1867. Built 1840–70. Designed by Sir Charles Barry and A. W. N. Pugin. Photograph by Stephen Ayling. Albumen print from wet collodion on glass negative. VAM 61.115.

18 The smoking room, Cecil Hotel, London, 1896. In the Indian style. The walls are covered with Doulton's tiles. Photograph by H. Bedford Lemere.

8. Pugin and principles

The completed New Palace of Westminster, which is still the largest secular Gothic Revival building in the world, was designed by the architect Charles Barry and the young A. W. N. Pugin, who provided most of the Gothic detail, both inside and out. Pugin's belief in Gothic as a style that could pull Britain back from the brink of social chaos has already been described. His theories were expanded in *The True Principles of Pointed or Christian Architecture*, published in 1841, which contained many of the ideas behind the subsequent treatment of the Gothic style. These went beyond a mere choice of period (although he favoured the 'Decorated' Gothic style of the early fourteenth century). Pugin urged architects and designers to work from the fundamental principles of medieval architecture and design. These included the banishing of features 'not necessary for convenience, construction or propriety' and the revealing of construction (but suitably beautified with ornament), so that a piece of architecture or design should clearly express its purpose, both symbolically and practically. This principle became a cornerstone of Victorian design reform.

In Pugin's own work, these ideas of truth to structure, function and material, and the rejection of 'sham' ('in God's house, everything should be real'), spread beyond architecture. They were applied to furniture in solid wood with revealed pegged construction, and to the employment of a group of manufacturers who could be trusted to make domestic and church furniture and fittings that obeyed his principles. As in architecture, correct ancient models were sought in furniture, metalwork and fittings, not only by Pugin, but also by the Ecclesiological Society, which adopted his ideas and applied them to reforming the interiors of existing churches, as well as influencing the form of new ones. In fact, from the 1840s church architecture and fittings were to take the lead in the Gothic style, culminating in the 1860s in a distinctive and very vigorous type of High Victorian Gothic. This rapidly departed from medieval precedent, taking on a particular nineteenth-century character.

19

19 *The Cartoon Gallery, Knole, Kent*, 1841. By Joseph Nash. Painted for his *Mansions of England in the Olden Time*, 1839–49. Watercolour. VAM 1037-1873.

THE GOTHIC REVIVAL

Jim Cheshire

During the Victorian period the Gothic style was transformed from an esoteric subject of Romantic contemplation to a major style in architecture and the decorative arts. For some 20 years, from the 1840s to the 1860s, it represented the cutting edge of high design.

The Victorian faith in the culture of the Middle Ages was exemplified early on by Lord Eglinton's re-creation of a medieval tournament at his Scottish castle in 1839. The event symbolized a strong feeling among Tory aristocrats that the utilitarian tendencies of the state had eroded patriotism and chivalry.

The architect Augustus Welby Northmore Pugin was a seminal figure in the history of the Gothic Revival, both as a theorist and as a practising designer. His key contribution was to give the Gothic style a moral impetus through arguments about the rationality of its construction. For Pugin, honesty of design lay in furniture or buildings that revealed their structure or supported the perceived essential properties of the material. These theories had direct stylistic consequences: furniture proudly proclaimed its construction with tusked tenon joints and huge decorative hinges, while veneer, non-structural ornament and 'Brummagen Gothic' were patently false.

21. *The Tournament at Eglinton*. By W. Gordon. From *An account of the tournament at Eglinton, revised and corrected by several of the knights*, 1839, by James Aikman. Published in Edinburgh by H. Paton, carver and gilder. Colour lithograph. VAM L.736-1937.

20. *Patterns of Brummagen Gothic*. From *The True Principles of Pointed or Christian Architecture*, 1841, by A. W. N. Pugin. VAM SC.94:0028.

22. Table, 1852–3. Designed by A. W. N. Pugin and made by John Webb of George Street, Hanover Square, London, for Francis Blanchard at Horsted Place, Sussex. Carved oak. VAM W.26-1972.

25. *Design for the Town Hall, Manchester*, 1867–8. By Alfred Waterhouse. Pen, ink and watercolour. VAM D.1882–1908.

23. Chalice and candelabrum. Designed by A.W.N. Pugin; the metalwork made by Hardman & Co., Birmingham. Left: chalice, Birmingham, with hallmarks for 1850–1. Made for the Great Exhibition, 1851. Champlevé enamels with silver, parcel-gilt and garnets. Right: candelabrum, about 1846. Made for the House of Lords. Brass. [h. 83.8cm]. VAM 1327-1851, 2742-1851.

24. *The Mediaeval Court*, 1851. By Louis Haghe. From *Dickinson's comprehensive pictures of the Great Exhibition of 1851*, 1854 (second edition; first published 1852). Printed and published by Dickinson Brothers, London, 1854. Colour lithograph. VAM 19536:15.

By the 1850s Gothic had gained momentum as a style for public buildings: all over the country Gothic churches were being built and Pugin's Medieval Court was acknowledged as a major success of the Great Exhibition. The critic John Ruskin was the great Gothic theorist of the 1850s: he saw Gothic buildings as evidence of the liberty of the craftspeople who made them. For Ruskin, this liberty had been destroyed by capitalism and Victorian Britain had a duty to restore this freedom to its artisans and artists. Pugin and Ruskin left a theoretical legacy that captivated a generation of Arts and Crafts designers later in the century, but in their hands these theories did not necessarily equate with the Gothic style.

William Burges is typical of the second generation of great Gothic designers: he had little of Pugin's religious or moral zeal and far wider aesthetic interests. Burges's taste was avant-garde: he collected Japanese prints and drew freely on designs from the Islamic world. All these influences are apparent in his extraordinary interiors, where the precise and serious symbolism of the Gothic Revival erupted into weird and wonderful fantasy schemes. As a Gothic designer he was too idiosyncratic to be really influential, but he remains a monument to the glorious disintegration of Gothic as the morally correct style in the later Victorian years.

26

27

26 Interior of the church of All Saints',
Margaret Street, London, begun 1849.
Designed by William Butterfield.

27 The Albert Memorial, London, built 1864–76.
Designed by Sir George Gilbert Scott.

28 *The Winter Smoking Room, Cardiff Castle,*
about 1870. By Axel Hermann Haig. The interiors
at Cardiff Castle, designed by William Burges,
were made from 1865 onwards. This room was
decorated as shown. Watercolour. The National
Trust, Knightshayes, Devon.

28

9. High Victorian Gothic

The tone for the style was set by the most famous of the ecclesiological churches, All Saints', Margaret Street, in London. Designed by William Butterfield and begun in 1849, it was built in the spirit of Gothic but without copying any particular details. Still standing today, its exterior is of uncompromising London brick and its interior is equally uncompromising, a shiny and almost violent display of machine-polished coloured stone and bright paint in strong patterns. The use of coloured stone, called 'structural polychromy', was first suggested in John Ruskin's *The Seven Lamps of Architecture*. Ruskin had studied its use in Italy, and its subsequent use in Britain ushered in a host of foreign Gothic ideas, which gave High Victorian Gothic its varied character. The machine-made ornament in All Saints' was also highly significant, for this type of Gothic was nothing if not frankly nineteenth-century, even accommodating exposed cast iron.

Perhaps the best-known example of High Victorian Gothic architecture today is Sir George Gilbert Scott's Albert Memorial, which was begun in 1864. Formed like a giant medieval shrine, it used in its decoration the same group of metalworkers, sculptors and others who had worked on the ornamentation and fitting-out of Scott's church work. It was from this group of Gothic architects and the medievalizing art-workers who supplied them with furniture, fittings, stained glass and textiles, metalwork and other furnishings that the first examples of painted 'art' furniture for the home emerged in the 1850s. They derived from medieval furniture and were plentifully supplied with painted decoration and metal trimmings. The most extreme exponent of this approach, the architect William Burges, was fortunate to find an immensely rich client in the mystically inclined third Marquess of Bute, for whom he created, from 1865, a number of extraordinary and completely furnished medieval fantasy buildings. Gothic art furniture of the 1850s developed during the next decade into a type of 'reformed Gothic' furniture, which matched contemporary Gothic architecture in its strong geometric lines and use of colour. Although a minority taste, reformed Gothic furniture played a major role in the earliest 'artistic' interiors of the 1870s, where it was combined with motifs from Japanese sources.

29

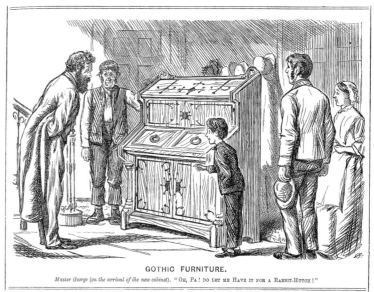

GOTHIC FURNITURE.

Master George (on the arrival of the new cabinet). "OH, PA! DO LET ME HAVE IT FOR A RABBIT-HUTCH!"

30

29 Cabinet, 1858. Designed by William Burges, painted by Edward J. Poynter and made by Harland and Fisher, London, for Herbert George Yatman. Pine and mahogany, painted and gilded. VAM Circ.217-1961.

30 *Gothic Furniture*. Cartoon from *Punch*, 18 November 1865. Ever ready to make fun of new styles, *Punch* here satirizes 'reformed Gothic' furniture. Wood engraving. VAM PP.8.L.

THE BATTLE OF THE STYLES IN THE HOME

Suzanne Fagence Cooper

Victorian designers had a bewildering diversity of styles at their disposal. Historical studies were developing apace, so it was possible for architecture and interiors to imitate classical, Renaissance or Gothic models more accurately. Past styles, moreover, could provide a reassuring appearance of stability and confidence at a time of disruptive social change. The introduction of Japanese and Middle Eastern elements into British design reflected new trading interests and commercial opportunities. London stores such as Liberty's imported exotic textiles, ceramics and metalwork to lend a modern artistic flavour to the drawing room. If a client wanted something more wholeheartedly British, then the simple shapes and restrained decoration of the Arts and Crafts workshops were ideal. The emphasis here was on skilled hand work, which sympathetically revealed the best qualities inherent in the raw material.

31. French-style grand piano, about 1840. Mechanism made by Erard & Co., London. Case designed and made by George Henry Blake for the wife of Thomas, Lord Foley, Baron Kidderminster. Satinwood marquetry with painted and gilded stand. [h. 95.3cm]. © 2003 The Metropolitan Museum of Art.

32. Egyptian-style upright piano, about 1870. Designed by William James and George Ashdown Audsley. Made in the workshop of W. H. and G. H. Dreaper. Ebonized wood, with carving, gilding and paint. National Museums and Galleries on Merseyside.

By the later years of the century all these styles, as well as some eclectic mixtures, battled for public attention in the displays and catalogues of department stores and furniture warehouses. A newly married couple could order a complete Old English dining room or a Louis XV boudoir from any number of Oxford Street stores.

33. The 'Manxman' piano. An Arts and Crafts-style upright piano designed in 1896 by Mackay Hugh Baillie Scott. Made in 1902–3, the mechanism by John Broadwood and Sons, London. Ebonized mahogany with carved wood, pewter, mother-of-pearl; marquetry of stained wood; silver-plated handles and hinges. VAM W.15-1976.

34. Arts and Crafts-style semi-grand piano, 1906–7. Designed by Sir Edwin Lutyens. Made by John Broadwood & Sons, London. Oak. VAM W.38-1984.

35. Oriental-style upright piano, with Japanese and Middle Eastern motifs, 1878. Designed by Henry W. Batley. Made by Collard & Collard, London; the case by James Shoolbred & Co., London. Carved boxwood. VAM W.26-1983.

Archetypal Victorian objects, such as pianos and teapots, were contorted to suit exotic or historical styles, however inappropriate they might be. With pianos, designers also had to wrestle with the problem of their unwieldy size and shape in their efforts to make them fit into their intended domestic surroundings. Technical improvements throughout the nineteenth century made the grandest instruments larger and more sonorous. It was only in the 1880s that design reformers returned to simplified shapes derived from harpsichords.

The piano provided a focus for Victorian social events, and particularly for female display. Consequently there was a strong incentive for the instruments to be lavishly decorated. They became a symbol of respectability among the aspiring middle classes. Wives and daughters relied on servants to do the household chores, so they had leisure time to spend at the piano. Richly decorated pianos dominated middle-class drawing rooms, signifying both their owner's taste and their social status. The eclectic range of motifs applied to these modern instruments – motifs whose origins ranged from the ancient past to the imperial present – represented one of the most distinctive elements of Victorian design.

36. Aesthetic-style grand piano, 1883. Designed by Sir Edward Burne-Jones. Decorated by Kate Faulkner. Made by John Broadwood & Sons, London. Oak, stained, with gilt and silvered gesso decoration. VAM W.23-1927.

10. The battle of the styles

The choice of Gothic for the Palace of Westminster did not go unopposed, and in fact marked the start of an architectural 'battle of the styles', a rivalry between classical and Gothic that ran up to the mid-1870s. It was seen most clearly in public buildings, where it reached its peak in the 1860s, with the newly established corporations of northern industrial towns building rival town halls: classical in Leeds, Gothic in Manchester. Even at the centre of government the battle raged, most famously over the Foreign Office in 1859, where Gilbert Scott was forced by the Prime Minister, Lord Palmerston, to replace his romantically towered Gothic scheme with an equally competent, if less romantic, Italianate scheme with an Osborne-like tower. The interiors were a blaze of colour in paint and stone.

In ecclesiastical architecture the styles divided along broadly denominational lines, with Gothic being chosen by the established Church, classical by the dissenters. The warehouses, offices and other commercial buildings rising in their hundreds in the burgeoning cities took full advantage of the elaborate eclecticism. Here, it was not a battle over principles but a battle for attention. In London at least the rivalry was welcomed by commentators, who saw the mixed styles and materials producing something like the variety seen in historical European city centres, in marked contrast to the plain uniformity (or tedium, as it was then seen) of the Georgian urban scene. In the City of London the classical dominated, with *palazzo*-like office blocks, but Gothic was especially favoured for warehouses, where its use for decoration was combined with cast-iron structures.

37

38

37 The Town Hall Leeds, West Yorkshire, built 1853–8. Designed by Cuthbert Brodrick.

38 The Town Hall, Manchester, Lancashire, built 1867–77. Designed by Alfred Waterhouse.

Perhaps the most vigorous supporter of the classical style was the government design reform machine itself, centred at the Museum and Government School of Design at South Kensington. Although the policy-formers of the South Kensington establishment had adopted many of Pugin's central ideas on design, they believed that Italian Renaissance, rather than Gothic, was the way forward for style, not simply because it included the best examples of the conjunction of art and manufacture, but because it most fully answered their ideas on the principles of design. The whole South Kensington complex from 1857 onwards was a built demonstration of the virtues of the North Italian Renaissance style, with elaborate coloured interiors in mosaic and ceramic in the same style (*see 3:22*). South Kensington largely failed to spread its brand of Renaissance beyond government buildings, but its adventurous experimentation with 'artistic' materials that would survive a corrosive urban atmosphere (notably strongly coloured brick and moulded terracotta), contributed a key element to the emergence of freer styles at the end of the century.

40

11. Art in the home

From about 1860 onwards ideas around the link between art and manufacture, and fine and decorative art, began to change in a way that had profound effects for the development of style. The activities of 'Art furnishers' promoted a new attitude towards design by producing furniture that was thought to have 'artistic' content. At first 'Art furnishing' was a minority taste, exemplified by the early work of William Morris and his associates, whose pioneering art-furnishing company was founded in 1861 as a direct result of Morris's inability to find sufficiently 'artistic' furniture for his own use in the commercial market. In the 1870s (and up to the end of the century) the word 'artistic' became a signal of the latest in design, led by the idea – as expressed in *Building News* in 1872 – that 'art and artistic feeling are as much shown in the design of furniture and other accessories as in what have hitherto been considered the higher or "fine" arts of sculpture and painting'. In architecture, too, 'artistic' ideas took hold among avant-garde 'art' architects, who thought of themselves more as artists (with studios) than as practitioners with drawing offices.

The artistic approach to design involved a highly eclectic and very free attitude to style. It also introduced, for the first time in fashionable interiors, the combination of antique and new furniture. Typically objects from Britain and abroad (and especially the Far East), and in a wide range of styles,

N.B.—The top of this Table is framed up of six pieces, producing a beautiful and varied effect of grain and colour.

The "Kenilworth"
Occasional Table,
in Walnut or Black Wood, very light and strong.
17/6

The "Medina"
Five o'clock Tea Table, of richly grained wood in "Liberty" Art Colours, with old Arab Musharabiyeh decoration.
95/-

The "Hampden"
Coffee Table,
strong and serviceable.
In Walnut or Black Wood,
10/6
In "Liberty" Art Colours,
15/-

Liberty & Co.]　　　[16]　　　[Regent Street, London.

39

39 Three occasional tables in the *Art Furniture* catalogue of Liberty & Co. of London, 1884. Occasional tables were a sure sign of the artistic. 'Kenilworth', in spite of its name, was Japanese in style; 'Medina' incorporated real Arabic elements; and 'Hampden', with its turned legs, was adopted from cottage furniture. Line-block. VAM Liberty Catalogues (4)-1884.

40 Design for a block of shops and offices, about 1855. By John Burley Waring. Built in iron and glass, with polychromy, in a variation on the Venetian Gothic style. Pencil, water and body-colour. VAM 830:1.

AESTHETICISM

Linda Parry

Aestheticism was a fashionable style of living developed in Britain between the 1860s and 1890s. Based on a philosophy of the importance of art above all, it became a significant movement in both literature and the visual arts. It was associated with a small but influential group of personalities, including the poet and writer Oscar Wilde and the actress Ellen Terry, whose work, dress and lifestyles helped form the style. However, it was artists such as J. M. Whistler and Aubrey Beardsley, and the designers E. W. Godwin and Thomas Jeckyll, who evolved the movement's elegant forms of design.

It was based on a number of historical and geographical sources, including Greek, Roman, Gothic and Georgian decoration, as well as the art of the Middle and Far East. The most important source was Japanese design, largely unknown to the West until the 1850s. Fashionable homes now displayed Japanese woodblock prints, screens, fans, blue-and-white china and rush matting as part of their decorative schemes, copying imaginative commissions by leading Aesthetic architect-designers such as Godwin and Jeckyll.

41. *Oscar Wilde*, 1882. By Napoleon Sarony. Albumen print. National Portrait Gallery, London.

42. Ornament from a railing, about 1876. Designed by Thomas Jeckyll. Made by Barnard, Bishop and Barnard of Norwich. Cast iron. [h. 77cm]. VAM Circ.530-1953.

Liberty's, the Regent Street shop, did much to popularize the style by selling imported goods as well as by manufacturing its own range of furnishings depicting popular Aesthetic motifs, such as peacock feathers, fans and sunflowers. By the end of the nineteenth century the Aesthetic style of decoration had crept into the design of many ordinary household items like wallpaper, china and clocks. Despite the fashion in Aesthetic dress for dull browns and sage greens, popular colours for the home included bright yellow, blue, and green highlighted with black and gold.

Many critics believed that Aestheticism was self-indulgent and superficial. The eccentric mannerisms and style of dress adopted by its followers were frequently lampooned in print. In 1881 it became the subject of Gilbert and Sullivan's comic opera *Patience*. With the publication of the first issue of *The Yellow Book* in 1894 criticism intensified. Designed and illustrated by Aubrey Beardsley, with contributions from many of the leading writers and artists of the day, this publication was instantly associated with the Aesthetic movement and, in turn, with what Victorian society considered the decadent and unacceptable lifestyles of its main exponents. Following Oscar Wilde's trial and imprisonment for homosexuality in 1895, Aestheticism never regained its popularity.

43. *Design for a display of Japanese-style furniture*, 1872–3. By Edward William Godwin. Pen, ink and watercolour. VAM E.482-1963.

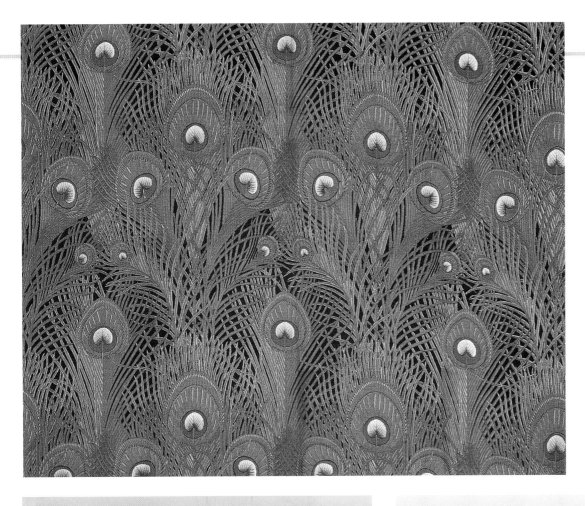

45. Detail of a clock, about 1880. Designed by Lewis Foreman Day. Made by Howell James and Co., London. Ebonized birchwood case with a porcelain face. VAM Circ.662-1972.

46. Printed cotton furnishing, *Peacock Feathers*, 1887. Designed by Arthur Silver (of the Silver Studio). Printed by the Rossendale Printing Co., Rossendale, Lancashire, for Liberty & Co. of Regent Street, London. Roller-printed cotton. VAM T.50-1953.

47. Greetings card, *May you have a quite too happy time*, 1882. Designed by Albert Ludovici, II. Printed and published by Hildesheimer & Faulkner, London. Colour lithograph. VAM E.2415-1953.

44. Poster for *The Yellow Book*, 1894. Designed by Aubrey Beardsley. Published by Elkin Mathews and John Lane at The Bodley Head, London. Line-block and letter-press. VAM E.1377-1931.

were combined in tasteful harmony. The rooms of pioneers like Morris's collaborator, the artist Dante Gabriel Rossetti, in the 1860s contained light Regency furniture and East Asian blue-and-white porcelain (both to become hallmarks of the artistic interior of the 1870s and 1880s) and an Egyptian-style sofa designed by Rossetti himself. The products of the Morris firm tended to be broadly medieval in character and drawn from sources as diverse as sixteenth- and seventeenth-century botanical book illustrations and Italian fifteenth-century textiles. However, they also included light furniture (some designed by Rossetti) taken from early nineteenth-century models. In architecture, as in interiors and furniture, there was a return to eighteenth- and seventeenth-century styles, with an emphasis on ordinary town and country building. These trends can be broadly divided into two main stylistic areas, although they often overlapped – namely the Aesthetic style and the Old English and Queen Anne styles.

48 *The sitting room at 16 Cheyne Walk, London,* 1882. By Treffy Dunn. Dante Gabriel Rossetti reads to Theodore Watts Dunton. The Regency furniture, paintings and chimneyplace were in the room by 1863. In the corner is a Morris & Co. chair. Watercolour. National Portrait Gallery, London.

49 'Daisy' wallpaper, the design registered in 1864. Designed by William Morris, and based on botanical illustrations. Made for Morris, Marshall, Faulkner & Co. by Jeffrey and Co. Block-printed in distemper colours. VAM E.442-1919.

49

12. Old English and Queen Anne style

The rediscovery of domestic vernacular architecture was the most significant stylistic development of the second half of the nineteenth century. It began in the 1850s, with houses by such architects as George Devey and the Gothicist William Butterfield, and with Red House, designed in 1859 by Philip Webb for William Morris. These were fundamentally medieval in style, but incorporated later ideas. The Old English style, developed in the 1860s by William Eden Nesfield and Richard Norman Shaw, established a freely composed type of building based on half-timbered Tudor vernacular. Also in the 1860s, at the peak of High Victorian Gothic, another style emerged, which combined ideas from a wide range of modest English and Dutch red-brick buildings of the seventeenth and early eighteenth centuries, using them in a free and informal way. The settled name of this comfortable, adaptable and extremely influential style was Queen Anne, although one of its earliest exponents, the architect John James Stevenson, preferred the name 'Free Classic' or even 'Re-Renaissance'.

51

50

50 *Design for Leyswood, Groombridge, Sussex,* 1868. By Richard Norman Shaw for James William Temple. Pen and ink. RIBA Library Drawings Collection.

51 Red House, Bexleyheath, London, built 1859–60. Designed by Philip Webb for William Morris.

The Queen Anne style, mixed in with Old English, was used in the famous 'artistic' suburb of Bedford Park, London, and in much urban building, ultimately leading to a form of public building in the 1890s taken directly from the grand baroque architecture of Sir Christopher Wren. The interior of a Queen Anne house in town might have rooms in styles that were seen as being appropriate to their function, such as a Jacobean hall and dining room, a neo-classical 'Adam-style' drawing room and a Moorish billiard room. But the rooms at Bedford Park tended to have artistic interiors in the Aesthetic style, mixing elements as diverse as Georgian decoration and exotic forms, most notably of Japanese origin.

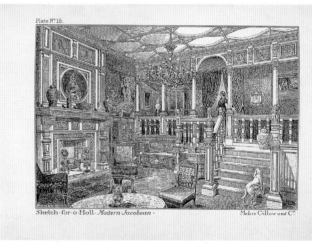

52 The Tower House and Queen Anne's Grove, Bedford Park, London, 1882. By M. Trautschold. Bedford Park, begun in 1876, contained buildings designed by a number of architects, but its style was set by Richard Norman Shaw, who designed the Tower House for the estate's developer, Jonathan T. Carr. Colour lithograph. VAM E.4039-1906.

53 *Sketch for a Hall. Modern Jacobean.* Plate from *Decoration and Furniture of Town Houses* by Robert William Edis, 1881. The Chinese jars and sunflower firedogs add an aesthetic touch. VAM 47.E.17.

54 Sideboard, 1867–70. Designed by Edward William Godwin, and made by William Watt and Co., London. A pioneering example of the Anglo-Japanese style. Ebonized mahogany, silver-plated metalwork and panels of embossed leather paper. VAM Circ. 38-1953.

13. Arts and Crafts and the morality of design

The Arts and Crafts movement marked the culmination of the trend towards morality in design that had begun with Pugin in the 1830s. Already by the 1850s the poorly made and sham had come to symbolize bad morals. The artistic movement of the 1870s believed strongly that the contemplation of beauty could by itself have a moral effect, making it possible for Lucy Orrinsmith, writing on interior decoration in 1878, to gush rather optimistically that 'it would be impossible to commit a mean action in a gracefully furnished room'. But for William Morris, the power of beauty was not enough. Although he was an art furnisher, his beliefs were fundamentally different from those of other art furnishers. He believed in the supremacy and moral worth of hand craftsmanship and in the central importance of the designer having a full understanding of the material in which he was designing. The ultimate goal was the general improvement of society.

By the 1880s these ideas had been taken up by a group of younger architects and designers, who had, like Morris, absorbed the notions of Pugin and Ruskin. In stylistic terms, however, they were very different from Morris.

Influenced by Queen Anne style and Aesthetic ideas, they rejected Morris's medieval complexity and deeply coloured richness for a lightness of tone and stylish clarity of outline that were both simple and sophisticated. Unlike the Aesthetic designers, however, their models were resolutely British and centred on the seventeenth and eighteenth centuries, identifying an English tradition of design that, in the words of the architect Arthur Blomfield in 1890, was characterized by 'steadfastness of purpose, reserve in design and thorough workmanship'. The results were often startlingly original, not least in architecture and interiors, which strove to leave behind the 'copyism' of the historicist approach and identify the essence of form. From about 1890 the architect C. F. A. Voysey developed a remarkably pure avant-garde style based on a few perfect forms and motifs impeccably executed, as did the designer Ernest Gimson. In describing Gimson's cottage around 1900, the engraver F. L. Griggs wrote, 'newly cut stone and oak, bright steel and glass, and white walls reflecting the sunshine, nothing but for use and comfort, and all without any sort of make-believe'. In Gimson's simple space, at the very end of the Victorian era, we have travelled very far indeed from the garish, ornament-filled interiors of 50 years before.

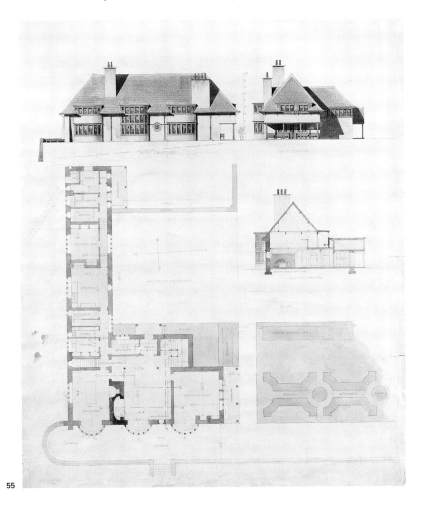

55 Design for Broadleys, Cartmel, Lancashire, 1898. By C. F. A. Voysey. Pencil and watercolour. VAM E.252.1913.

56 *Music Room in a House at Crowborough*. By M. H. Baillie Scott. Illustration from *The Studio*, vol. 26, 1902, p.117. Colour halftone. VAM P.P.73.A.

57 The interior of Ernest Gimson's cottage at Sapperton, Gloucestershire, about 1904. The armchair was designed by W. R. Lethaby, the table by Gimson himself.

ARTS AND CRAFTS

Linda Parry

Arts and Crafts was an approach to manufacture as well as a style. It developed in Britain during the last quarter of the nineteenth century and took its name from a society formed by a group of artists, designers and craftspeople keen to exhibit their work and provide a forum for the exchange of ideas.

The first exhibition of the Arts and Crafts Exhibition Society was held in London in 1888. It covered all aspects of art and design, from architecture, paintings and sculpture to furniture, textiles, ceramics, glass, metalwork, book binding and illustration, gesso, mosaic,

calligraphy and typography. The work, which was by both amateurs and professionals, was very varied in design, but a strong underlying philosophy controlled the way in which all the exhibits were designed and made. In time, this led to the characteristic style of the Arts and Crafts movement.

Galvanized by William Morris's ideas on the democratization of art and the importance and pleasure of work, Arts and Crafts

58. *The dining room at the Magpie and Stump, 37 Cheyne Walk, London,* the house of C. R. Ashbee, 1901. Interior designed by Ashbee. Attributed to Fleetwood C. Varley. Pencil and watercolour. VAM E.1903-1990.

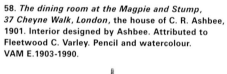

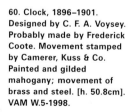

59. Armchair, 1892–1904. Designed and possibly made by Ernest Gimson. Made in Pinbury or Sapperton, Gloucestershire. Ash, turned on a pole-lathe, with splats of riven ash; the rush seat is a replacement. VAM Circ.232-1960.

60. Clock, 1896–1901. Designed by C. F. A. Voysey. Probably made by Frederick Coote. Movement stamped by Camerer, Kuss & Co. Painted and gilded mahogany; movement of brass and steel. [h. 50.8cm]. VAM W.5-1998.

exponents increasingly turned away from large, mechanized factories as their main means of manufacture. Instead they set up small workshops, which concentrated not on speed and economy, but on the practical skills of the workers and the pleasure derived from craftsmanship. Importance was placed on the natural beauty of materials. Simple structures and techniques were used that would help to highlight these qualities. Many traditional methods of manufacture were revived. Just as the practice of specialized small-scale production emulated that of medieval guilds, so a nostalgia for the vernacular traditions of the British countryside provided the main inspiration for the design of Arts and Crafts houses, both inside and out.

Many Arts and Crafts followers also sought to live a simple country life, moving out of towns and setting up workshops in rural areas. Some went to areas that could supply the materials for their particular needs. Frequently this provided much-needed work for a local workforce no longer able to secure a living from the land.

Although the style was associated with the countryside, the movement had a strong cosmopolitan base. Many leading exponents were based in cities, and its popularity continued to spread through shops such as Liberty's, which adopted the style as its own. By the end of the century Arts and Crafts ideals had infiltrated the design and manufacture of all the decorative arts in Britain, while its influence in Europe and America was also gaining ground.

61. Washstand, about 1894. Probably designed by Leonard F. Wyburd, for the Liberty Furniture Studio, London. Tiles designed and decorated at the pottery of William De Morgan. Oak with iron fittings and ceramic tiles. [h. 121cm]. VAM W.19-1984.

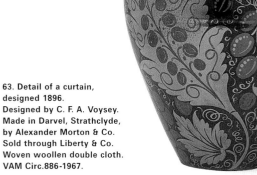

62. Vase and cover, 1888–98. Designed by William De Morgan and decorated at the De Morgan pottery, Sand's End, Fulham, London. Earthenware, painted in lustre on a blue background. [h. 30.4cm]. VAM C.413-1919.

63. Detail of a curtain, designed 1896. Designed by C. F. A. Voysey. Made in Darvel, Strathclyde, by Alexander Morton & Co. Sold through Liberty & Co. Woven woollen double cloth. VAM Circ.886-1967.

14. Art Nouveau and the Glasgow School

The last significant stylistic development of Queen Victoria's reign took place in Glasgow in Scotland, where a remarkable group of architects and designers, including Charles Rennie Mackintosh, Margaret and Frances Macdonald and Herbert MacNair, came together in about 1893. They devised a new style, which was the closest that advanced British design came to continental Art Nouveau. In fact, Art Nouveau was one of their sources, but others included medievalizing British painting, continental symbolist art, the drawings of Aubrey Beardsley and the designs of C. F. A. Voysey, while their general approach was profoundly affected by the Arts and Crafts movement.

Mackintosh's architecture was a brilliant synthesis of Gothic, old Scottish and other ideas, best shown in his Glasgow School of Art, begun in 1897. Although its work was celebrated abroad, the Glasgow group's influence on British design was small. Together with the Arts and Crafts style and continental Art Nouveau, it fed into the synthetic style, which in the 1890s became the trademark of the London department store of Liberty & Co. The products of the Arts and Crafts movement, and indeed of Liberty's, reached only the upper middle classes. For the rest, all the styles shown in the 1851 Exhibition were still available in their infinite variety.

64 Sheet of sanitary (washable) wallpaper, the design registered in 1895. Made by the firm of David Walker, Middleton, Lancashire. The design combines rococo, Jacobean, classical and naturalistic motifs. Sanitary papers were intended for halls and kitchens, their cheapness making them widely used. Colour-printed from engraved rollers. VAM E.1943-1952.

65 Chair, made about 1900. Originally designed in 1897 by Charles Rennie Mackintosh for Miss Cranston's tearooms, Argyle Street, Glasgow. This example is from a set made for Mackintosh's Glasgow flat. Stained oak; modern upholstery. VAM Circ. 130-1958.

66 The Glasgow School of Art, first phase, 1907–9. Designed by Charles Rennie Mackintosh.

66

65

67

67 The ladies' drawing room, King's Head Hotel, Sheffield, 1902. An interior in the mixed modern style promoted by Liberty & Co. The chairs carry Glasgow School rose motifs, the cabinet is inspired by Voysey and an Art Nouveau dish is on the table. Photograph by H. Bedford Lemere.

3289

3290

3291

3292

3293

3294

3295

3296

3297

3298

3299

3300½

CHAPTER 3

Who led taste?

MICHAEL SNODIN

1. Finding the way

Walk down any antiques market, or leaf through any Victorian shop catalogue or journal, and one of the most characteristic features of the Victorian age is immediately apparent: its staggering range of visual choice. How did the Victorians navigate through this immense quantity of ingenious elaboration? In fact there was no shortage of people eager to help; more ink being spilt on the subject of taste in Victoria's reign than at any time before or since. Commentators included weighty critics like Ruskin, Morris and Pugin, newly professionalized architects and designers, journalists, novelists, interior decorators, teachers, exhibition, museum and gallery organizers, and those who formed government design policy.

In contrast to previous eras, the majority of these putative taste makers were professionals with an axe to grind. Most were reacting to what they saw as a crisis in design, triggered by the end of the old, classically based certainties of the 'rule of taste' linked to an ordered society. These certainties were, they felt, unsustainable in the face of stylistic proliferation, social change and ever-cheaper goods. The resulting confusion was all too easily filled by manufacturers happy to make what the public wanted. Those critics who tried to seize control of the situation believed that the old idea of high design as an expression of social authority had evaporated; on the other hand, it was now available to a huge public and, with the added uplifting ingredient of art, had the potential to be an influence for good in the broadest sense. Although they disagreed, sometimes violently, in their fundamental aims and solutions, all the critics believed that taste had to be controlled – for the good of the consumer, the good of the maker and, ultimately, the good of the nation.

This moral and social imperative set apart the taste-making processes of Victorian Britain from what came before. That is not to say that many of these processes did not have earlier beginnings. The commercial drive that produced the Victorian department store differed only in scale from the great shopping advances of the Regency. Design-conscious art manufacturers, like the potters Minton and Doulton, were building on earlier examples such as Wedgwood and the Regency goldsmiths Rundells. Government design reform initiatives from the 1830s represented the culmination of a century of fitful attempts to raise national design standards in the economic battle against imported manufactured goods, especially those that came from France. The mechanisms of these reforms, the official design schools, the museums of applied art and the various attempts to establish national design standards were, however, entirely new.

The nature of patronage of architecture and design was also shifting. Firstly, compared with the years before 1837, patrons were becoming less important, as architects and designers set themselves up as a professionalized group of self-appointed and self-publicizing taste makers. Rich families with old money, like the Dukes of Devonshire at Chatsworth, who had consumed advanced taste in the past, tended to become conservative, pursuing historicist styles and rarely employing leading designers or architects. The Marquess of Bute, for whom the architect William Burges devised complete medieval environments, was a notable exception (*see 12:28*). Some of the newer rich, like the Rothschild family, favoured the French style, an international symbol of modern, but conservative, luxury. On the other hand, many newly

1 Detail of a page from the *Glass and China Book*, published by Silber and Fleming Ltd, of London, 1880–90. Colour lithograph. VAM A.20.16.

moneyed manufacturers, merchants and entrepreneurs became significant collectors of art, especially in the 1870s and 1880s.

Sir William Armstrong of Newcastle, inventor, engineer and armaments manufacturer, built the great country house of Cragside and filled it with the works of Albert Moore and Dante Gabriel Rossetti, while the Liverpool ship owner Frederick Leyland fitted into his London house the Peacock Room, the most famous Aesthetic-style interior. But such patrons were in the end far less significant leaders of taste than their more modest middle-class counterparts, among whom there were many artists, like William Morris (whose Red House was the focus of design activity by several of his friends) and J. M. Whistler (whose studio house, which was designed by E. W. Godwin, was too radical for the local government officials of the Metropolitan Board of Works).

2

3

2 The south drawing room, Halton House, Buckinghamshire, 1892. The house was finished in 1886 for Alfred de Rothschild, a notable collector of pictures. Photograph by H. Bedford Lemere.

3 The Peacock Room at 47 Prince's Gate, London, 1892. Designed by Thomas Jeckyll and painted by James McNeill Whistler for the shipbuilder Frederick R. Leyland. Photograph by H. Bedford Lemere. Albumen print. VAM PH.240-1926.

4 Design for the White House, Chelsea, London, 1877. By Edward William Godwin. This design was turned down by the Metropolitan Board of Works, which made Godwin add more ornament. Watercolour, pen and ink. VAM E.540-1963.

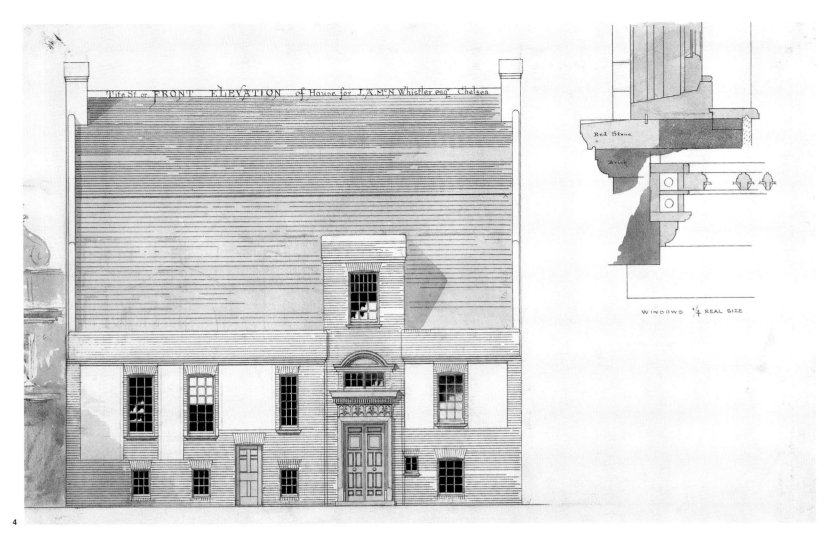

Tite St or FRONT ELEVATION of House for J.A.McN Whistler esq. Chelsea

Red Stone

Brick

WINDOWS 1/4 REAL SIZE

4

In an age of grandiose public building, public patronage also played a key role in the formation of taste. At South Kensington the government design establishment attempted to create, by example, a classical national style. A newly revived Church of England inspired a mass of building, restoration and furnishing. Other public bodies, like the London School Board, also played a role. Its 'beacons of light' in some of London's poorest districts were built (at least externally) in the very new, 'Queen Anne' style – a symbol of a better lifestyle, which was designed to appeal to the middle-class ratepayer and stamp a clear brand on the school enterprise. While the moral effect on the children is unknown, the schools certainly helped to spread the Queen Anne style to local house builders.

5 The London Board School, Gloucester Road, Camberwell, London, opened in 1875. Designed by Edward Robert Robson. Greater London Photographic Library.

5

THE CHURCH

Jim Cheshire

Ecclesiastical design was a burning issue for the Victorians. The range of design solutions to the differing denominational demands is aptly illustrated by the contrast between Pugin's idealized interior of 1844 and the 'Tabernacle' built for the immensely popular Baptist preacher Charles Haddon Spurgeon between 1859 and 1861.

The architectural focus of Spurgeon's church is the pulpit – appropriate for a form of worship where the sermon is the focal point of the service. The auditorium seated 6,000 people. The architectural and aesthetic focus of a Puginian church is the east end, where the density of ornament signifies the sacrament of the Eucharist: the focus of the Roman Catholic Mass.

6. *An Altar hung for a Funeral Mass*. Lithographed by H. C. Maguire after A. W. N. Pugin. From *Glossary of Ecclesiastical Ornament and Costume* by Pugin, 1844. Colour lithograph. VAM G.58.G3.

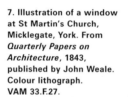

7. Illustration of a window at St Martin's Church, Micklegate, York. From *Quarterly Papers on Architecture*, 1843, published by John Weale. Colour lithograph. VAM 33.F.27.

8. Left: chalice, with London hallmarks for 1867–8. Designed by William Burges. Made by Jes Barkentin of Barkentin & Krall, London. Silver-gilt, enamels, semi-precious stones and stained glass. [h. 21.4cm]. Background: altar frontal, 1875. Designed by J. P. Seddon. Made by a professional embroiderer for St Andrew's, Wells Street, London. Woven silk damask and velvet embroidered in floss silks in long and short, satin and stem stitches with couched Japanese gold thread, seed pearls and metal ornaments. Right: missal, 1870. Designed by George Henry Birch. Made by Jes Barkentin. Binding: parcel-gilt with enamels and gems. VAM Loan: Kingsbury. 1-1985, Loan: St Andrews.1, Loan: Kingsbury.3.

Attitudes within the Church of England covered almost the whole spectrum between these two poles. The new radicals of the Oxford Movement stressed the Roman Catholic roots of the Anglican Church; their sympathizers in Cambridge took it upon themselves to invent ecclesiology: the 'science' of church building. This combined

9. Tiles: The Evangelists, about 1845. Designed by A. W. N Pugin. Made in Stoke-on-Trent, Staffordshire, by Minton & Co. Earthenware with inlaid decoration. [h. 43.4cm]. VAM C.81-1976.

10. Ecclesiastical cope and hood, 1848–50. Designed by A. W. N. Pugin for use at St Augustine's Church, Ramsgate, Kent. Made in London and Birmingham. Silk velvet with velvet appliqué, surface embroidery in silks, with raised, padded and couched work in silks and silver-gilt wire, and thread. VAM T.289–1989 and T.287-1989.

the theology of the Oxford Movement with Pugin's theories and transformed them into churches and church furniture. Opponents of the Oxford Movement, mainly Evangelicals, favoured worship closer to Spurgeon's principles than to Pugin's and portrayed ecclesiological innovations as dangerous and sometimes even illegal. Controversies raged throughout the Victorian period, eventually redefining the relationship between the state and the Church, with the state gaining the upper hand.

Thousands of churches were built or restored by all denominations, but it was the densely decorated churches promoted by ecclesiologists that provided much of the market. Church work surged in the 1840s, but probably did not peak until the 1870s, providing a wealth of opportunities for architects and designers of metalwork, stained glass, tiles and church furniture. The amount of money raised from private sources was enormous. An increased demand for commemorative and memorial products fitted in well with ecclesiastical products and provided numerous commissions for manufacturers and designers.

During the 1840s journals and books were important in disseminating the new stylistic vocabulary demanded by the increasingly discerning ecclesiastical patron. Ecclesiological societies and commercial publishers produced hundreds of images of historical sources, which the designers transformed into distinctly Victorian products.

With hindsight, we can see many of the developments in Victorian religion as heralding the gradual secularization of British culture, but to the Victorians theirs was the great age of church building, and for us it remains an important period of ecclesiastical design.

11. *Interior of the Metropolitan Tabernacle, London* (detail), 1861. Designed by W. Wilmer Pocock. From *The Builder*, 4 May 1861. Engraving. VAM PP.19.G.

2. Art and commerce

In 1857 Sir Thomas Acland, a friend of John Ruskin, wrote there were 'at least three parties contending in England for the mastery of guidance in the arts'. Firstly, there was the Royal Academy, in which 'the traditions of the past and the tastes of the dilettanti find expression'. Secondly, the Government Schools of Design, with their 'doctrinaire adherence to abstract principles'. Thirdly, there was 'Mr Ruskin and his pre-raphaelite allies – a considerable force of irregulars'. The last two represented the main reactions to the Victorian design crisis. The government design establishment thought that the answer to taste control lay in working with the forces of commerce through a rational programme, although manufacturers, with a keener sense of what the market would bear, were reluctant allies. Ranged against them was a fundamentally anti-commercial tendency, of which Ruskin and Morris were a part, which worked on broader cultural lines, believing in the power of art to transform society. At the start of the Victorian period the first group had the upper hand; by the end, the second was in control. In practice the efforts of both groups were more or less compromised by their reliance on rigid standards of taste, which completely failed to take into account the complexities of a mixed market. Most consumption of visual culture continued to lie outside the charmed circle of the visually approved.

Two of the tangible results of Victorian government involvement in national design issues, and what we would now call design politics, are still with us: the Victoria and Albert Museum, successor to the South Kensington Museum, and the Royal College of Art, whose ancestor, the Government School of Design in London, was founded in 1837. Both the school and the museum, which was originally attached to it, came out of the report of a Parliamentary Select Committee on the arts and their Connexion with Manufactures. It sat in 1835 and 1836, partly to investigate the Royal Academy and partly to 'enquire into the best means of extending the knowledge of the arts and the principles of design among the people (especially the manufacturing population) of the country'. Although the establishment of the Committee should be seen in the context of the general tendency towards enlarging education provision that followed the Great Reform Act of 1832, its main purpose was to improve the design quality of British manufactures in the context of moves towards free trade. The Committee's conclusions were predictable. Witness after witness (including manufacturers, retailers and artists) 'felt themselves compelled to draw a comparison more favourable (in the matter of design) to our foreign rivals, and especially the French, than could have been desired'. Only a system of design schools, both in London and in the manufacturing towns, could, it was asserted, solve the problem.

The resulting London design school – pioneering in the British context – was modelled on those in Germany and France and was appropriately enough run by the Board of Trade. Provincial schools survived only as far as they were supported by local manufacturers. From the start there were problems, principally because of resistance to attempts to limit the schools' teaching to the applied arts, but gradually a curriculum emerged in the London school, which taught (at least in theory) the history and principles of ornament. The arrival in the mid-1840s of Henry Cole transformed the situation, not only of the schools, but also of public visual education in Britain.

12

12 Teaset, designed 1846, made 1846–71. Designed by Henry Cole for Felix Summerly's Art Manufactures. The set was awarded a silver medal by the Society of Arts. Made by Minton & Co., Stoke-on-Trent, Staffordshire. Earthenware. VAM 2741-4-1901.

3. Henry Cole and Prince Albert

Even in an age of great men, Henry Cole was an extraordinary figure. Before 1849 he had played a key role in reorganizing the public records and setting up the Penny Post. He applied a similar single-minded approach to his next project, which was nothing less than the reformation of national design and design education along rational and utilitarian lines. To that end he set up his own manufacturing enterprise (Felix Summerly's Art Manufactures) and a propagandizing magazine (the *Journal of Design and Manufacture*) and was the key figure, with Prince Albert, in staging the Great Exhibition. Following that triumph, and after much characteristic manoeuvring behind the scenes, Cole was given control of the School of Design and its museum. With the establishment of the Department of Practical Art and the move of both school and museum to South Kensington, he was able to achieve his ideal.

The 'South Kensington System', a centralized system of art and design education, extended beyond the London school to provincial design schools and right down to elementary schools. Consistency was assured by a rigid curriculum centred on abstract drawing exercises and a scheme of national prizes. The whole system was based on the set of simple and rational design 'principles' formalized by Cole and his team, notably Richard Redgrave and Owen Jones. They were also used in the arrangement, design and decoration of the South Kensington Museum (and its associated institutions in Dublin and Edinburgh), turning them into demonstrations 'by which all classes might be induced to investigate those common principles of taste, which may be traced in the works of excellence of all ages'.

GENERAL PRINCIPLES OF DECORATIVE ART.

The true office of Ornament is the decoration of Utility. Ornament, therefore, ought always to be secondary to Utility.

Ornament should arise out of, and be subservient to Construction.

Ornament requires a specific adaptation to the Material in which it is to be wrought, or to which it is to be applied; from this cause the ornament of one fabric or material is rarely suitable to another without proper re-adaptation.

True Ornament does not consist in the mere imitation of natural objects; but rather in the adaptation of their peculiar beauties of form or colour to decorative purposes controlled by the nature of the material to be decorated, the laws of art, and the necessities of manufacture.

PUBLISHED BY CHAPMAN AND HALL, 193, PICCADILLY, LONDON.

13 Detail of a plate from *The Drawing Book* by William Dyce, 1842. Dyce, a painter, was Superintendent of the London School of Design. Lithograph. VAM 15561:a 2.

14 Prize drawing of a plaster cast, 1840. Made by R. W. Herman at the Government School of Design. Black and white chalk. VAM E.1967-1909.

15 One of eight placards on design, published by the Department of Science and Art in 1853. They were hung up in the classrooms of the Government School of Design. VAM 52.D.68.

THE GREAT EXHIBITION OF THE WORKS OF INDUSTRY OF ALL NATIONS

Paul Greenhalgh

The Great Exhibition of 1851 transformed everyone's vision of what an exhibition might be. The world's first large-scale temporary international exhibition, or 'expo', it aimed to bring together as complete a range as possible of manufactured produce, across the arts and sciences. Staged in Hyde Park inside the legendary Crystal Palace, a giant iron, wood and glass structure, the exhibition ran for six months from 1 May. It had 6,039,195 visitors, of whom 4,439,419 paid the minimum one-shilling entrance fee. The public were particularly enthralled by the displays of technology, with working steam engines, and by the extraordinary display of raw materials and artworks gathered from the nations in the British Empire.

By the time the exhibition closed it had generated a profit of £186,000, a vast sum in those days. These profits were used to pay for a succession of international exhibitions throughout the century and to found museums at South Kensington, including the Victoria and Albert Museum.

16. *Aeronautic View of The Palace of Industry For All Nations*, 1851. By Charles Burton. Published by Ackermann & Co., London. Colour lithograph. VAM 19614.

Though funded mainly by the private sector, the Great Exhibition was in reality a government initiative to improve standards of design in British manufacturing and to educate the public in matters of taste. The 'taste makers' responsible for it were not a sophisticated aristocratic élite, as they might have been in previous centuries, but civil servants, manufacturers and art teachers. Committed simultaneously to the improvement of manufacturing industry and to the general public, many of them thought that the way forward was to fuse art and industry.

17. *The Agricultural Court*, 1851. By an anonymous artist. Published by Lloyd Brothers & Co. and Simpkin Marshall & Co., London. Colour lithograph with hand colouring. VAM 19538:25.

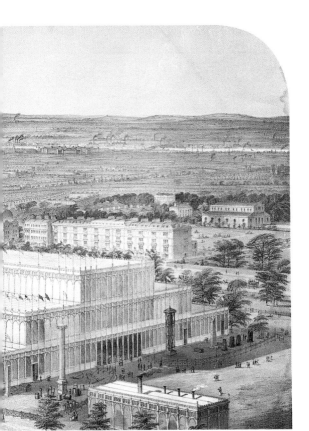

18. *The Indian Court*, 1852. From *Dickinson's comprehensive pictures of the Great Exhibition of 1851*, 1854 (second edition; first published 1852). Printed and published by Dickinson Brothers, London, 1854. Colour lithograph. VAM 19536:11.

19. Pair of vases, about 1851. Made by Charles Meigh & Son, Hanley, Staffordshire, and exhibited at the Great Exhibition of 1851. Stoneware with relief moulding and painted decoration in enamels and gilding. [h. 101.6cm]. VAM Circ.374-1963 and Circ.418-1963.

20. *The Crystal Palace Transept after the close of the exhibition*, 1852. By Benjamin Brecknell Turner. Albumen print from waxed paper negative. VAM PH.1-1982.

Since 1851 the Crystal Palace itself has consistently been recognized as an architectural masterpiece. Pioneer modernist Le Corbusier looked back on it as the first true work of modern architecture. In contrast to the elegant construction of the building and its delicate ornamental detailing, the objects displayed inside were widely thought to be vulgar and tasteless. Critics then – and later – saw this gathering of high Victoriana as an artistic disaster.

The Great Exhibition triggered a period of design reform in Britain. As a result of the exhibition, art and design criticism grew dramatically as a profession, the taste of its salaried critics being characterized by a rejection of complex, eclectic decoration and an embracing of simpler surfaces and restrained profiles. It seems that positive lessons were taken from the building and negative ones from its contents.

21

23

The buildings were designed in the recommended northern Italian Renaissance style and demonstrated technical experiments in new building materials. Like contemporary churches, their interiors carried instructive and edifying images and mottoes tailored to the contents of the rooms. The whole was a determined attempt to bring high design and high art to the widest possible public.

The most precious objects at South Kensington were, by the late 1860s, contained in a memorial gallery to the Prince Consort. This was entirely appropriate, for Prince Albert was the fairy godfather of the whole enterprise. While Queen Victoria reflected rather than led national taste, Prince Albert worked actively to bring about design reform, linking it to his interest in science and technology. Within the royal sphere, he set an example as a collector and patron of art and architecture. He was also a designer in his own right, conceiving a silver centrepiece and the influential royal seaside villa, Osborne House on the Isle of Wight. The Prince's Germanic taste and foreign connections brought to England experts from abroad, who carried with them advanced theoretical ideas about art and design. These included the art historian Ludwig Gruner and the architect and art-

22

21 The original entrance front of the South Kensington Museum, London, built 1864–6. Designed by Captain Francis Fowke. The terracotta decoration was designed by Godfrey Sykes.

22 *View of the ceramic gallery, South Kensington Museum, London*, 1876–81. By John Watkins. The gallery was designed by F. W. Moody and Godfrey Sykes, and created in 1867–9. The frieze and columns carried names of potters and factories; the stained-glass windows showed ceramic manufacture. Etching. VAM E.370A-1900.

23 Tazza, commemorating the life and work of Prince Albert, 1863. Designed by John Leighton. Made in Stoke-on-Trent, Staffordshire, by William Taylor Copeland. Engraved by Charles Henry James. Glazed earthenware, transfer-printed. [h. 12.8cm]. VAM 715-1899.

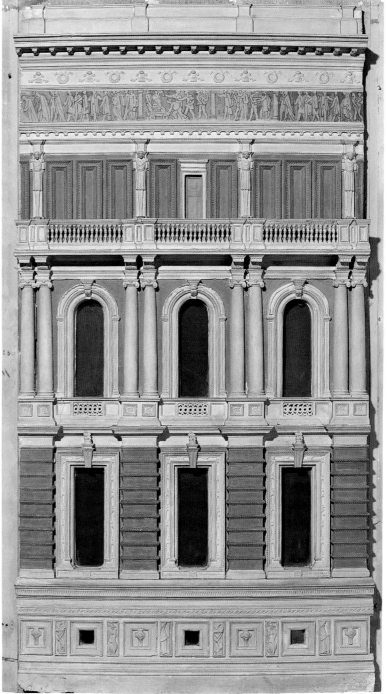

historical theorist Gottfried Semper, who taught at the Government School of Design and designed the Duke of Wellington's great funeral car, as well as a neo-Renaissance scheme for South Kensington in 1857. In the event, lack of cash killed Semper's scheme, 'very much . . . to the Prince's disappointment'. When permanent buildings did go up in the 1860s, they were in the Semperian manner, albeit designed by officers of the Royal Engineers.

In the end, however, the Prince was most significant as a committee chairman leading the key design events of the 1840s and 1850s. In 1843 he became chairman of the largely dormant Society of Arts, turning it (together with Cole) into an engine that eventually produced the Great Exhibition of 1851. He was also involved in the Dublin exhibition of 1853 and the Manchester Art Treasures exhibition of 1857. But Prince Albert's greatest contribution was the conception of the idea of 'an establishment, in which, by the application of Science and Art to Industrial pursuits, the Industry of all nations may be raised in the scale of human employment', making permanent the ideals of the Great Exhibition. Bought with the profits of the Exhibition, South Kensington (itself a new name) became such a centre, incorporating art, science and natural history museums, colleges, the Royal Horticultural Society gardens and the Albert Hall, as well as a succession of international exhibitions. Most of the numerous buildings reflected the official style.

24 Sgraffito plaster decoration on the Science Schools, South Kensington (now the Henry Cole Wing, Victoria and Albert Museum). Designed by F. W. Moody and carried out by students of the Art School, formerly the Government School of Design, 1872. Contemporary photograph. VAM Picture Library.

25 Model for the façade of the Royal Albert Hall of Arts and Science, London, 1868. By Major-General Henry Young Darracott Scott. Officers from the Royal Engineers led the building activities at South Kensington. The hall was opened in 1871. Plaster. VAM A.11-1973.

THE SOUTH KENSINGTON MUSEUM

Karen Livingstone

The South Kensington Museum opened in 1857 and was the first public institution in Britain to try to educate directly an audience of students, manufacturers and the general working public through its diverse collections of contemporary art, manufactures and historical decorative art. Its foundation was the result of 20 years of progressive effort to improve standards of taste and manufacture in Britain. Under the administration of Henry Cole and his joint secretary, the artist Richard Redgrave, the museum grew beyond its origins as part of the government initiative to train students of design.

From about 1840 a collection of objects was formed for the Government School of Design, augmented by objects from the Great Exhibition, selected to demonstrate excellence of manufacture. In 1852 the school and museum moved to Marlborough House, where the newly appointed Cole promoted the museum's aim of improving taste by employing a series of principles of art. Tunisian textiles, for example, demonstrated the successful distribution of form and harmony of colour. Cole contrasted these 'true' examples of manufactures with a celebrated but short-lived display of 87 examples of 'False

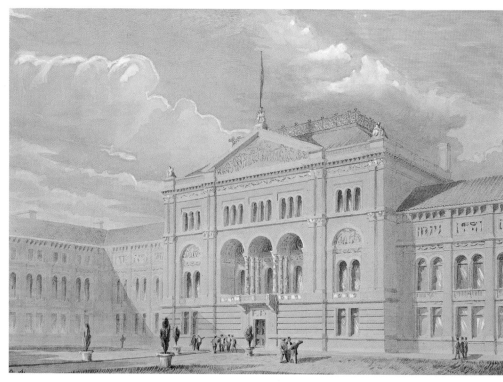

27. Detail of *Sketch for the north side of the quadrangle of the South Kensington Museum,* **1860. By Captain Francis Fowke. Watercolour. VAM E.1318-1927.**

Principles in Decoration', to illustrate where British manufacturers were going wrong. The 'chief of the vices' was the 'direct imitation of nature', as illustrated by exhibit 16, a 'furniture chintz' imitating ribbon and roses on a flat surface and lacking symmetrical arrangement.

The main focus of the museum's collections soon began to shift from modern manufactures to medieval and Renaissance decorative arts. Important private collections were purchased or lent to the museum, including the comprehensive Soulages collection. Despite criticism that this kind of historical collection would be of little benefit to manufacturers, some (including the pottery manufacturer Herbert Minton) can be said to have taken inspiration from them.

In 1857 the museum moved to South Kensington, adopting a new name and restating its purpose as the democratic

26. *Henry Cole and Richard Redgrave,* **1854. Attributed to Charles Thurston Thompson. Albumen print. VAM PH.835-1987.**

28. Two jugs. Top: late 16th century. In the manner of Bernard Palissy, from the Soulages collection. Lead-glazed earthenware, moulded with applied decoration. [h. 27.5cm]. VAM 7178-1860. Bottom: 1858. Modelled by Hamlet Bourne. Made in Stoke-on-Trent, Staffordshire, by Minton & Co. Earthenware, majolica glazes. VAM 4730-1859.

education of taste. Evening and weekend opening ensured that working people were able to visit. At this date the displays were not confined to works of art. A wide range of displays could be seen, including an Educational Museum, Patented Inventions and Products of the Animal Kingdom. Plans were rapidly laid for new buildings and by about 1860 the South Kensington Museum was presenting a grand public façade, turning itself into a national decorative-arts institution with far-reaching influence.

30. Objects from the School of Design collection and the Museum at Marlborough House. From left to right: Iznik bottle, about 1600. Made in Turkey. Earthenware. Indian 'Bidri ware' cup with lid, about 1851. Probably made in Bidar, India. Blackened zinc alloy overlaid with silver (bidri). Pilgrim bottle, about 1560. Made in Castel Durante or Urbino, Italy. Tin-glazed earthenware. Bottle, about 1844. Made by Frederic-Jules Rudolphi. Chased, oxidized silver, parcel-gilt. Vase, about 1840. Made by E.-D. Honoré, Paris. Porcelain. VAM 973-1875, 151-1852, 8409-1863, 919-1844, 3101-1846.

31. *A Room at Marlborough House with the Soulages collection on display*, 1857. By William Linnaeus Casey. Watercolour. VAM AL.7280.

32. Detail of a sash, about 1851. Made in Tunisia. Woven silk. VAM 808-1852.

29. Detail of a furnishing fabric, English, about 1850. This 'furniture chintz' was exhibit 16 in the 'False Principles' display. Roller-printed cotton. VAM T.6-1933.

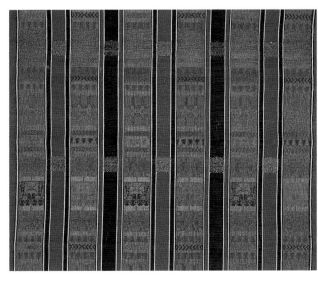

4. Did South Kensington work?

The efforts of the government design machine had mixed results. They undoubtedly brought art and design to large numbers of the upper artisan class, as well as the middle classes, and in purely social terms this was truly innovatory. As Henry Cole wrote in 1857:

> In the evening, the working man comes to this Museum from his one or two dimly lighted, cheerless, dwelling rooms, in his fustian jacket, with his shirt collars a little trimmed up, accompanied by his threes, and fours and fives of little fustian jackets, a wife, in her best bonnet, and a baby, of course, under her shawl. The looks of surprise and pleasure of the whole party when they first observe the brilliant lighting inside the Museum show what new, acceptable, and wholesome excitement this evening entertainment affords all of them.

But the positive effects in terms of taste were less easy to quantify. In the field of architecture and decoration, the South Kensington buildings were intended to act as a testbed for new forms and techniques. While their dominant neo-Renaissance style in ceramic and iron was emulated in a few hotels and public buildings, the untypical Dutch Kitchen or Grill Room by Sir Edward Poynter and William Morris's Green Dining Room were in the end far more significant, pioneering in the 1860s later forms of aesthetic decoration. In promoting its design principles among manufacturers, South Kensington also had mixed success. Cole claimed that by seeing objects of good taste, the general public would demand more of these goods, eventually persuading manufacturers into supplying better products. The same effect was to be achieved by directly educating manufacturers, designers and manufacturing artisans in the principles of good design.

34

33

Among consumers, however, progress was not very great. In wallpaper and textiles, for instance, the quite considerable production of approved flat-patterns, after designs by Pugin and Jones, during the 1850s and 1860s hardly dented the popularity of the naturalistic and illusionistic 'French' papers and fabrics, which had been singled out for attack in Cole's short-lived display of False Principles (an exhibition that had to close after opposition from the manufacturers). Nor did Cole's mechanistic 'principles', even though they were partly derived from Pugin, impress critics of South Kensington, like Ruskin and Charles Dickens. In a famous passage in his novel *Hard Times*, Dickens has Cole, thinly disguised as the schoolmaster Thomas Gradgrind, making a little girl cry because she is not allowed to admire the apparently real flowers in the carpet. For Ruskin, the very idea of a rule-bound system offended his notions of architecture and decorative art springing naturally from the mind of the craftsperson in direct relationship with nature.

---

33 *The Grill Room, South Kensington Museum, London*, 1876–81. By John Watkins. The room was designed by Sir Edward Poynter and begun in 1866. The tiles were painted by a class of female students at the Art School, formerly the Government School of Design. The stove, dated 1866, was decorated with Japanese motifs. Etching. VAM E.815-1945.

34 Detail of a furnishing fabric, about 1850. Made in Lancashire, possibly for Jackson and Graham, Furnishers of London. Shown at the Great Exhibition, 1851, and in the display of 'False Principles in Decoration', 1852, as an example of 'Direct imitation of nature': it showed a 'general want of repose'. Roller-printed and glazed cotton. VAM T.11-1933.

35 The Green Dining Room or Morris Room, Victoria and Albert Museum, London. Designed by Phillip Webb, with stained glass and painted panels by Sir Edward Burne-Jones. Decorated by Morris, Marshall, Faulkner & Co, 1866–8.

In raising the consciousness of art, however, and in helping to establish 'art manufactures' (made by 'art workmen') as a distinct type of visual culture, South Kensington had a considerable effect. This concept was entirely new. It elevated the applied arts from mere fashionable furnishings and decorations, subject to shifting patterns of taste, to a new type of high design, distinguished by its incorporation of the ennobling and morally purifying element of art. In the process, high design threw off its role as a social indicator subject to the whims of fashion. It became just as appropriate – or perhaps even more so – in the public context of a church, museum or exhibition as in the home. By contrast, the applied arts of the century leading up to 1850 were seen (at least up to the 1870s) as particularly defective, products of a period when a debased classical style served a frivolous and fashion-dominated aristocracy. The most admired periods were the medieval (as favoured by Pugin, Ruskin and Morris), the Renaissance (South Kensington and the Art Schools) and the golden 'Olden Time' of the Tudors and Stuarts, which had seized the popular imagination as early as the 1820s. All combined the attraction of a pre-industrial, benevolent age, when styles were generated naturally rather than adopted, fashion was (it was believed) unknown, and art existed for its own sake: 'they made it to keep, and we [make it] to sell', as Ruskin wrote.

37 *Augustus Welby Northmore Pugin*, 1845. By John Rogers Herbert. Oil on canvas. Palace of Westminster.

37

38

Linked to this rediscovery was an investigation of ancient methods of making. The leaders in this process were art manufacturers and furnishers, like the potters Minton and Doulton, the metalworkers Hardman and the decorating firm of Crace, who rediscovered old techniques in the fields of pottery, tiles and enamels, and stained (rather than painted) glass and textiles. One interesting outcome was that the manufacturing element often cost far more than the materials, making art manufactures except in precious metals inappropriately expensive. This affected William Morris, who always regretted that his hand-methods inevitably meant that his products were only 'ministering to the swinish luxury of the rich'.

The art manufacturers were spurred on by architects, with whom they often worked in close collaboration, turning churches and public buildings into lavish demonstrations of the art workman. The pioneering figure in this trend was A. W. N. Pugin, who, with other architects, employed Herbert

36

36 Vase, 1867. Designed and modelled by Victor Etienne Simyan and painted by Thomas Allen. Made by Minton & Co., Stoke-on-Trent, Staffordshire. The technique and some motifs imitate 16th-century maiolica. One of a pair bought by the South Kensington Museum for £158.10 in 1871. Earthenware, painted in enamels and majolica glazes. [h. 121.9cm]. VAM 1047-1871.

38 The 'Paradise Lost' shield, 1867. Made by Leonard Morel-Ladeuil for Elkington & Co. It was shown at the Exposition Universelle, Paris, in 1867, winning Morel-Ladeuil a gold medal. Bought by the South Kensington Museum, London, in 1868. The theme was taken from John Milton's *Paradise Lost*. Silver and damascened iron. [h. 87.6cm]. VAM 546-1868.

Minton and chose John Hardman, an obscure button manufacturer, as his chief metalworker. Pugin was also the first architect-designer to make the critical leap from commissioned work to the production of designs for general use. He encouraged J. G. Crace to make and sell his furniture, wallpaper and carpets; as he wrote in 1847: 'We must have a turn at *carpets* next. Let us reform them altogether.' Two years later Pugin was promoting his furniture, reassuring Crace: 'Rely on it, the great sale will be articles that are within the reach of the middling class . . . I am so anxious to produce a sensible style of furniture of good oak, & constructively put together that shall compete with the vile trash made & sold.'

39

39 House of Lords Chamber, Palace of Westminster, London, designed from 1844, completed 1852. Designed by Sir Charles Barry and A. W. N. Pugin.

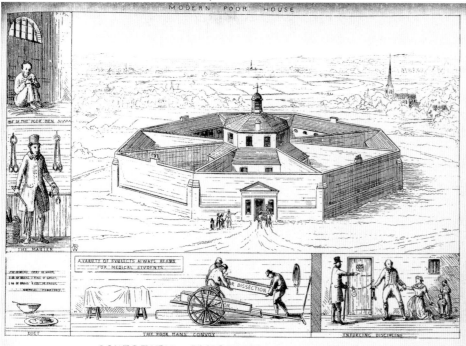

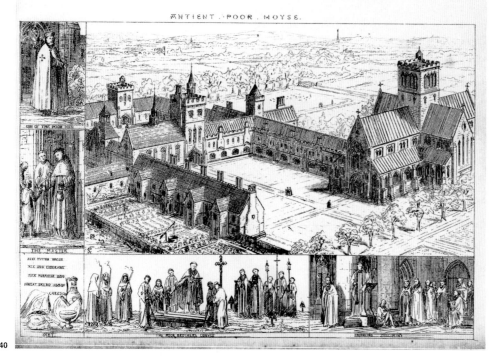

5. Pugin and Ruskin

'I was awakened from my slumber by the thunder of Pugin's writings,' wrote the architect George Gilbert Scott, looking back to the 1830s. The impact of Pugin's brilliant illustrated polemics was far greater than that of his comparatively few built schemes or the products designed by him. For Scott, Pugin's *Contrasts* 'vividly exposed the abject meanness which pervaded the architecture of the day', while *True Principles* 'established a code of rules founded on common sense, utility and truth'. Pugin himself said in 1851 that 'my writings have revolutionized the taste of England'. He was correct, for with Ruskin he was the most influential writer on design of the Victorian period. He was the first to tackle the Victorian style crisis, made Gothic the leading style of the period up to 1870 and introduced the key ideas of honesty in design and workmanship – what he called 'reality' – into Victorian design thinking. The fundamentally religious, indeed sectarian, position of Pugin's ideas did not impede their spread. Several of his central tenets fed into the secular and aggressively utilitarian atmosphere of the government design reform. In the hands of the Anglican reformers of church aesthetics in the Ecclesiological Society (founded as the Cambridge Camden Society), they were turned into a set of rules far more rigid than anything out of South Kensington. The laws were extended beyond buildings in the approved style to fittings and liturgical vessels, transforming the visual language of the established

40 *Contrasted Residences for the Poor*. Plate from *Contrasts* by A. W. N. Pugin, 1836. VAM Loan: Clive Wainwright.

41 John Ruskin, 1894. Photograph taken in Brantwood, Cumbria, by Frederick Hollyer. Salt paper print. VAM PH.7603-1938.

religion in thousands of churches, old and new. Pugin's most significant effect in the long term was on a generation of Gothic architects coming to maturity in the 1850s, like William Morris's collaborator Philip Webb (not to mention Morris himself), setting in train a development that ultimately led to the emergence of the Arts and Crafts movement in the 1880s. The other key figure in this development was John Ruskin.

42

In spite of the notoriously changing nature of his ideas, the subtle eloquence with which Ruskin set them out made him a powerful influence in many fields. On a purely stylistic level there was his advocacy of north Italian Gothic, notably in *The Stones of Venice* (1851–3), as the way out of the Victorian stylistic impasse. This not only led to many buildings being built in the style, but also opened up British architecture to foreign Gothic styles in general, including northern French Gothic, as promoted by the architect Eugène Viollet-le-Duc. Although Ruskin's aesthetic beliefs were rooted in the Christian faith, he preached against Gothic as a purely ecclesiastical style. The civic and commercial nature of many of the Gothic buildings that he studied legitimized modern Gothic in such buildings as town halls and warehouses and in domestic architecture: 'I have had indirect influence on nearly every cheap villa-builder between this [Denmark Hill, his home] and Bromley,' he wrote in 1872.

As an adviser on taste, Ruskin was much in demand. In 1864 he was called to Bradford to lecture on architecture at a time when the style of the town's new Exchange was being decided. In the end he was displeased with the chosen building and altered the printed version of his lecture to reflect his view: 'You may know there are a great many odd styles of architecture about; you don't want to do anything ridiculous; you hear of me, among many others, as a respectable architectural man-milliner; and you send for me, that I may tell you the leading fashion; and what is, in our shops, for the moment, the newest and sweetest thing in pinnacles.'

It was Ruskin's anti-industrial and anti-rationalist approach to aesthetics, rather than his advocacy of a particular style, that had the greatest impact on future developments. His direct appeal to the heart, and his belief in the reforming power of a personalized art and hand-craft based on a study of nature, influenced people as diverse as William Morris, leaders of the Aesthetic movement like Edward Godwin and Oscar Wilde, and members of the Arts and Crafts movement into the years after 1900. Certain texts were more important than others; as Morris wrote about 'The Nature of Gothic' from *The Stones of Venice*: 'To my mind, and I believe to some others, it . . . will be considered one of the very few and inevitable utterances of the century.'

42 *A window of the Palazzo Foscari, Venice*, 1845. By John Ruskin. Made in preparation for *The Stones of Venice*, 1851–3. Pencil and watercolour on paper. VAM D.1726-1908.

43 *The Nature of Gothic*, 1892. By John Ruskin. Printed by William Morris at the Kelmscott Press, Hammersmith, London. Woodblock engraving and letter-press. VAM 95.C.26.

43

The degree to which Ruskin's ideas on hand manufacture filtered through to a more general level is shown in the sales literature of commercial church furnishers. In about 1859 Cox and Sons, as 'church furniture manufacturers', were boasting of their Patent Carving Machines, through which, thanks to the wonders of technology, ' . . . the work is roughed out with great accuracy and expedition (the Cutter making seven thousand revolutions per minute), while the finishing of the more minute parts is carried out by hand labour, so that the result shows precisely the same amount of artistic excellence as if it had been entirely executed by hand'. By 1872 Cox's had subtly shifted the emphasis towards hand manufacture, even though the method of making was probably the same: ' . . . it is desirable to explain that it [the carving machine] is used solely for the purpose of preparation, by the removal of superfluous parts of the material, and shaping it for subsequent hand carving . . . without the artistic excellence of the work being in the slightest degree impaired'.

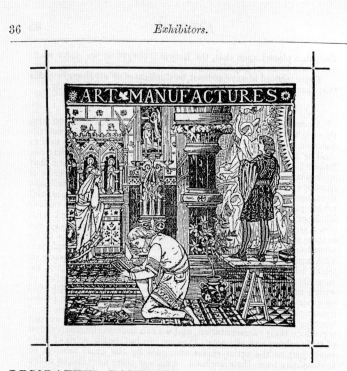

36   *Exhibitors.*

ART MANUFACTURES

DECORATIVE PAINTERS,
EMBROIDERIES,
METAL WORK,
STAINED GLASS,
TEXTILE FABRICS,
WOOD AND STONE CARVING.

COX, SONS, BUCKLEY, & CO.

28 and 29 SOUTHAMPTON STREET, STRAND, LONDON, W.C.

Specimens of Modern Venetian Table Glass,
manufactured by Salviati & Co.

45

6. The Art movement

Cox's change of heart need not have come from a direct reading of Ruskin. The early 1870s saw the emergence into public consciousness of the Art movement, characterized by a new concern to achieve beauty in everyday life, driven by a new wave of literature. Within 10 years aestheticism had become a popular fashion (as well as an object of popular ridicule), a development marked by Gilbert and Sullivan's operetta *Patience* and by the publication of one of the first books to record a contemporary artistic movement as such, Walter Hamilton's *The Aesthetic Movement in England* (1882). Hamilton's analysis was clear: 'the essence of the movement is the union of persons of cultivated taste to define and decide upon what is to be admired'. Given such unpromising beginnings among a tiny clique of artists, architects and self-proclaimed aesthetes, and its very loose nature, the movement's success among the middle classes may at first seem surprising. Nor does the positive tone of most Aesthetic literature suggest that it would be any more effective in changing tastes than the bossy material coming out of South Kensington. The secret of its success was that it was concerned largely with the domestic in architecture and interior decoration and that it was chiefly aimed not at the general public but at a small group of like-minded, moderately wealthy middle-class people wishing to join the exclusive club of the artistic. In a typical piece of polemic of 1881–2 in *The Burlington* magazine the imaginary Mr Philistine Jones, whose dazzling carpets and wallpapers of 1870 'were enough to give a templar a fit of delirium tremens', ' . . . actually has begun to think about the shape of his jugs'.

The pioneering book of the Art movement was Charles Locke Eastlake's *Hints on Household Taste in Furniture, Upholstery and Other Details* (1868). Eastlake's newly coined term, 'Art Furniture', expressed the crucial shift from

44 Advertisement for Cox, Sons, Buckley & Co., London. From the *Handbook to the Ecclesiastical Art Exhibition*, London, 1881. VAM 217.D.21.

45 *Specimens of Modern Venetian Table Glass. Manufactured by Salviati & Co.* From *Hints on Household Taste in Furniture, Upholstery and Other Details* by Charles Locke Eastlake, 1868. VAM 47.E.13.

individual art manufactures to art applied to the interior as a whole. The book's heady and pioneering mix of a discursive text along Puginian and Ruskinian lines with firm practical and illustrated decorating advice for every aspect of the house drove it to four British editions up to 1878, and six in America between 1872 and 1879. Eastlake set the tone and approach for all the rest, even though the styles they promoted changed considerably, shifting from Eastlake's Gothic to the 'Chippendale'-style furniture of the 1870s. Significantly most of the later books, like those in the *Art at Home* series, were written by women, from the same social group as their audience. Two, Rhoda and Agnes Garrett, were professional interior decorators (then a new career for women); the rest were often linked to artists and the Art movement, such as Lucy Crane (sister of Walter, and author of *Art and the Foundation of Taste*, 1882) and Lucy Orrinsmith (sister of William Morris's associate Charles Faulkner, and author of *The Drawing Room, its Decorations and Furniture*, 1878). Their mixture of aesthetic and practical household advice placed such works close to the growing genre of books of domestic advice, from Mrs Beeton onwards. The two genres actually merged in the hands of slightly later authors, like Jane Panton, author of *From Kitchen to Garret* (1889) and many other books.

7. Commerce and artist

These developments went hand-in-hand with huge growth in commercial outlets of artistic design. These ranged from manufacturers of a single product type, like Doulton's or the Linthorpe art potteries, to art furnishers in general, like Morris and Co., William Watt and Liberty and Co. This growth was matched by an increasingly public profile of individual designers. The example set by Pugin, as both a designer and a journalist and critic on design subjects, was followed by many later avant-garde art designers intent on spreading their ideas, including Owen Jones, Christopher Dresser and E. W. Godwin.

Some manufacturers exploited the links with such avant-garde designers. In the case of William Watt, the firm's links with the pioneering aesthetic designer and architect E. W. Godwin were fully publicized. Its stand at the Paris Exposition of 1878 was jointly designed by Godwin, painted by J. M. Whistler, clearly marked with their names and given the provocative title 'Decorative Harmony in Yellow and Gold'. Such a stunt could not fail to draw attention. The type of close aesthetic control exercised by both Godwin and Whistler, in this and other projects, was matched at a more general level by a tendency for art manufacturers to present their wares in complete settings, both in their showrooms and in illustrated catalogues. Watt's *Art Furniture*, originally published in 1877 with text and illustrations by Godwin, had a design influence far beyond its direct sales function: it was even available in the South

46

46 *View of a Drawing-Room*. Plate from *Suggestions for House Decoration in painting, woodwork and furniture* by Rhoda and Agnes Garrett, 1876. From the *Art at Home* series. VAM 47.D.40.

47

47 The William Watt stand at the Exposition Universelle, Paris, 1878. Painted by James McNeil Whistler and designed by Edward William Godwin. Photograph by Usine Photographique de Pallencourt, under the direction of H. Klerjot. VAM Picture Library.

Kensington loan scheme for books for art schools, joining such basic texts as Owen Jones's *Grammar of Ornament*.

Concerns about originality and authenticity, which lay behind the Design Registration Acts of 1839–43, became especially acute when named designers came to the fore in the 1870s. One solution, the addition of facsimile signatures or other marks of authenticity, was indicative not only of the designers' view of themselves as artists, but of their desire to keep control of the object. Such marks were also exploited by manufacturers. In the case of Doulton Art Pottery, which hired decorators directly from the South Kensington Schools, all the designers had their own mark. Christopher Dresser saw to it that the wide range of products he designed carried his facsimile signature as well as the usual design registration marks. The double function of his signature as an assurance of art value and a means of personal promotion was made clear by the wording of the 1879 prospectus and share certificate of the Linthorpe pottery. This was set up as a producer of cheap pottery at the suggestion of Dresser, who became the firm's 'Art Designer and Art Superintendent': 'Dr Dresser's name, as is well known, is inseparably connected with Art and Designing, and all articles proceeding from the Linthorpe Art Works will bear the facsimile of his Signature, "Chr Dresser" as a trade mark and guarantee of their genuineness, and of their being made in strict accordance with the principles of decorative Art.' Interestingly, in Linthorpe's case, the magic of Dresser's name seems not to have done the trick, for in 1882 the firm turned to less adventurous designs.

49

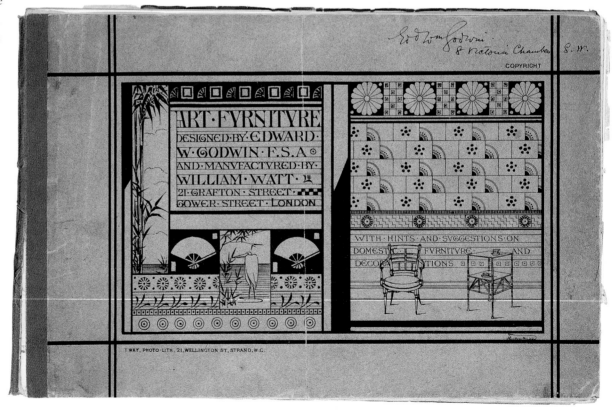

48

48 *Art Furniture designed by Edward W. Godwin FSA and manufactured by William Watt*, 1877. VAM AAD.4/508-1988.

49 Vase, 1882. Modelled by Harry Barnard for Doulton & Co., Lambeth, London. Salt-glazed stoneware. [h. 26.5cm]. VAM C.54-1972.

8. Taste and the Arts and Crafts movement

The Arts and Crafts movement could not have happened without the heightened aesthetic consciousness of the 1870s. From the start, however, the movement was much more coherent in its ideas and their presentation than the loose trends of that decade. The official history of the movement is a rather dry tale, beginning in the early 1880s, of societies and guilds of like-minded aesthetes, designers and architects. It accurately reflects the movement's essence, but signally fails to reveal its anti-establishment fervour and the larger-than-life characters that pushed it forward. Ruskin's writings, backed up by the example and ideas of William Morris, were the touchstones of the movement's artistic and social creed. Ruskin had a personal influence on pioneers like the architect and designer Arthur Heygate Mackmurdo. Mackmurdo, Ruskin's companion and assistant in 1874, went on to co-found the Century Guild in 1882. It was created in direct homage to Ruskin's own medievalizing Guild of St George, a group dedicated to rendering 'all branches of art the sphere no longer of the tradesman but of the artist'. The movement acquired a coherent public face, and a name, with the foundation of the Arts and Crafts Exhibition Society in 1887, which grew out of the Art-Workers' Guild, founded in 1884. The Ruskin Reading Class at the philanthropic Toynbee Hall in London's impoverished East End led to the movement's most daring experiment in social engineering, Charles Robert Ashbee's Guild of Handicraft, made up of working-class men and lads from the area.

51 Design for the symbol of the Arts and Crafts Exhibition Society, 1888. By George Heywood Sumner. Pen and ink. VAM E.1097-1993.

52 Salver, with London hallmarks for 1896–7. Designed by Charles Robert Ashbee. Made by the Guild of Handicraft, Essex House, London. Silver. VAM Circ.471-1962.

50 Chair, 1881. Designed by Arthur Heygate Mackmurdo. Probably made by Collinson and Lock, London. A chair of this type was shown by the Century Guild at the International Invention Exhibition in 1885. Mahogany, with an inset fretwork panel; replacement leather upholstery. [h. 97.2cm]. VAM W.29-1982.

50

WILLIAM MORRIS

Linda Parry

William Morris (1834–96) was one of the most influential of all Victorians. He was a celebrated poet, author and translator, a political activist and one of the early pioneers in the movements concerned with the conservation of ancient buildings and the countryside.

His artistic achievements were equally wide-ranging. Not only was he one of the most popular interior decorators of the nineteenth century, but he and his firm were responsible for designing, making and selling all of the furnishings – stained-glass, wallpapers, tiles, furniture, embroidery, woven and printed textiles, carpets and tapestries – used in his interior schemes. However, his art was not restricted to decoration of the home. A keen calligrapher in his early life, his last artistic endeavour was the founding of the Kelmscott Press, one of the most important private presses of modern times.

53. Detail of jasmine wallpaper, first issued 1872. Designed by William Morris. Printed by Jeffrey & Co. for Morris, Marshall, Faulkner & Co. Block-printed in distemper colour. VAM E.475-1919.

54. *William Morris*, 1877. The London Stereoscopic Co. National Portrait Gallery, London.

As his reputation as a designer and manufacturer spread through the work of the firms of Morris, Marshall, Faulkner and Co. and, from 1875, Morris & Company, so did his influence on all aspects of the decorative arts. Firms began copying his manner of work, reverting to small units using traditional manufacturing techniques, many of which had disappeared in the earlier years of the nineteenth century in the race for economic and technological expediency. Similarly, fellow designers, keen to capture the simplicity of Morris's floral patterns, turned to the British countryside for their inspiration.

Morris's views on art and life, clearly set out in numerous publications and lectures, found an even wider audience. His belief in the intrinsic value and joy of craft work, and in the need for equality of opportunity, was widely applauded by the new intellectual élite, who were becoming politically sensitive and keen to champion new causes. But his influence also spread to official channels. Morris gave evidence at government inquiries set up to look into the future of art education and the development of industry in Britain.

55. Detail of curtain of *Peacock and Dragon* woven furnishing, 1878. Designed by William Morris. Made by Morris & Company. Hand-loom jacquard-woven woollen twill. VAM T.64-1933.

57. The Hall at Red House, Bexleyheath, London, 1859–60. Designed by Philip Webb for William Morris and decorated by Morris.

58. Sussex armchair, designed about 1860. Possibly designed by Philip Webb. Made in London by Morris, Marshall, Faulkner & Co., and later by Morris & Company. Ebonized beech with a rush seat. VAM Circ.288-1960.

Furthermore, as one of the major advisors to the South Kensington Museum for more than 20 years, he suggested which acquisitions represented the best from the past and were, therefore, most useful for study by the designers of the future.

By the late nineteenth century Morris's reputation as one of the most original designers and thinkers of his day had gained wide international recognition. His London shop became a place of pilgrimage for visitors from throughout Britain, Europe, North America, Scandinavia and Australia. His ideas continued to influence the development of the arts in the twentieth century, both at home and abroad.

56. *The Works of Geoffrey Chaucer*, 1896. Designed by William Morris with illustrations by Edward Burne-Jones. Engraved on wood by William Harcourt Hooper. Printed at the Kelmscott Press, Hammersmith, London. VAM L.757-1896.

59. Detail of panel of tiles from Membland Hall, Devon, designed 1876. Designed by William Morris. Made by the firm of William De Morgan. Decorated in Chelsea, London, using tile blanks supplied by the Architectural Pottery, Poole, Dorset. Hand-painted enamels on earthenware. VAM C.36-1972.

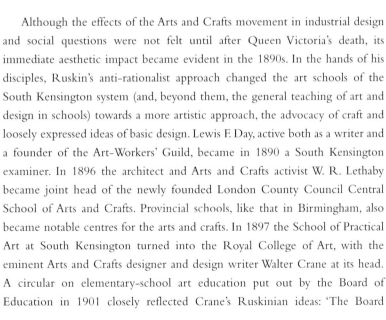

regard instruction in drawing as an important means of cultivating in children a faculty of observing, comparing, recollecting and thinking about all sorts of objects with a view to representing them in an intelligent and careful manner and developing a sense of beauty.' No greater shift from the dry mechanistic exercises of William Dyce's *Drawing Book* of 1842 could be imagined (*see 3:13*). A similarly profound shift from the rule-bound systems of South Kensington is shown in the relaxed approach to pattern design of the architect C. F. A. Voysey, writing in 1896 to the textile manufacturer Alexander Morton on the principles of what he called 'breadth'. Breadth was 'literally the proportion of one scale of richness to another One colour to another One mass to another One curve to another . . . Breadth is on the side of simplicity and repose.'

Public interest in the decorative arts and in the hand-made was shown and promoted in a range of new magazines. Art manufactures had of course long been discussed and illustrated in art magazines. The pioneering *Art Journal* (founded as the *Art Union* in 1839) not only regularly showed and illustrated manufactures, but also published catalogues of the great international

Although the effects of the Arts and Crafts movement in industrial design and social questions were not felt until after Queen Victoria's death, its immediate aesthetic impact became evident in the 1890s. In the hands of his disciples, Ruskin's anti-rationalist approach changed the art schools of the South Kensington system (and, beyond them, the general teaching of art and design in schools) towards a more artistic approach, the advocacy of craft and loosely expressed ideas of basic design. Lewis F. Day, active both as a writer and a founder of the Art-Workers' Guild, became in 1890 a South Kensington examiner. In 1896 the architect and Arts and Crafts activist W. R. Lethaby became joint head of the newly founded London County Council Central School of Arts and Crafts. Provincial schools, like that in Birmingham, also became notable centres for the arts and crafts. In 1897 the School of Practical Art at South Kensington turned into the Royal College of Art, with the eminent Arts and Crafts designer and design writer Walter Crane at its head. A circular on elementary-school art education put out by the Board of Education in 1901 closely reflected Crane's Ruskinian ideas: 'The Board

60 'Panpipes' furnishing fabric, late 1890s. Designed by C. F. A. Voysey, made by Alexander Morton and Co. Woven silk, cotton and wool, double cloth. VAM T.169-1977.

61 Poster for *The Studio*, 1893. Designed by Aubrey Beardsley. Line-block and letter-press. VAM E.451-1895.

exhibitions. But the tone of such journals was largely informational. The Aesthetic movement also produced its own journals, such as *The Burlington* and *The House, An Artistic Monthly for Those who Manage and Beautify the Home* (begun in 1897). The crucial shift was towards journals that promoted the avant-garde and put the fine and applied arts on an equal footing as two sides of the same coin. The most important of these was *The Studio*, founded in 1893. From the start it took an overriding interest in avant-garde applied arts and design, publicizing new work to a wide audience at home and abroad (an American edition began in 1897). But the real influence of this and similar magazines is perhaps most clearly indicated by the arrival of advanced styles in the sphere of commercial furnishing, especially through the firm of Liberty & Co.

62 Cover of the programme for
The Mikado, Savoy Theatre, London,
1885. Colour lithograph.
VAM Theatre Museum.

9. High style goes commercial

Liberty's approach to the commercial promotion of progressive design, and its failure to champion exclusively the hand-made, caused C. R. Ashbee to call them 'Messrs Nobody, Novelty & Co'. Arthur Lasenby Liberty, the founder of the firm, was not a designer but a merchant adventurer and entrepreneur in the old mould. He began in the great shawl and cloak emporium of Farmer and Rogers, setting up an oriental warehouse with purchases from the 1862 exhibition. He became deeply committed to the Art movement, with which he became linked in 1875 through his independent project, East India House, described by Godwin the following year as the 'Anglo Japanese warehouse'. In an astute publicity move, Liberty supplied the textiles for the costumes for Gilbert and Sullivan's *Patience* and was involved in the costumes for *The Mikado*. In 1883 he set up a new shop, selling textiles, furniture and furnishings as well as eastern goods. A year later a costume department was added, with Godwin as consultant, for the sale of artistic 'rational' dress, in direct opposition to conventional fashion. Like the other departments of the shop,

R. D'OYLY CARTE, Proprietor and Manager.

62

the overt aim of 'the new school of dressmaking' was the education of taste, producing its own informative booklets on styles in historical dress. However, it also had a commercial purpose, for it used Liberty's own fabrics, which were too soft for the usual run of dressmakers working in the stiff fashions of Paris.

What made Liberty's exceptional as a department store was its creation, by the 1890s, of a complete package of advanced good taste in a style so unified and distinct that 'Stile Liberty' could become an alternative name for Art Nouveau. One of the keys to this achievement of brand image was the concealment of its designers, many of whom were famous names. Only through such methods could Liberty's produce a style that would respond quickly to the market and tone down the extremes of innovation.

64

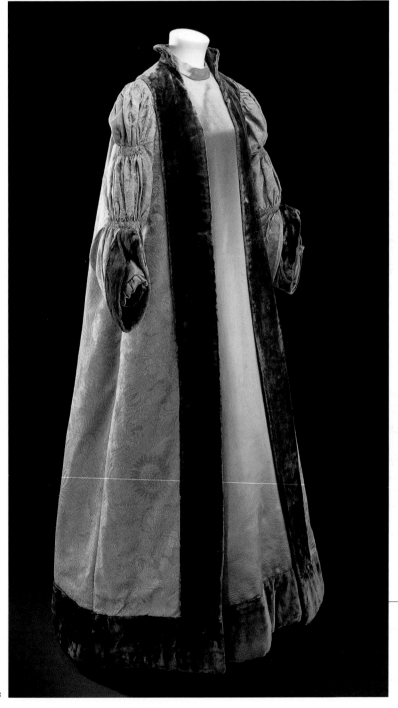

63

The great department stores of late Victorian England were the clearest demonstration of the overwhelming range of goods available by 1900, spread by a great tide of commercial propaganda. The type of branded taste control exercised by Liberty's was exceptional, with most other stores aiming to show the largest possible range of goods in the greatest number of styles. Whiteley's in London was known as the Universal Provider. In 1887 it was described in *Modern London*: 'Whiteley's is an immense symposium of the arts and industries of the nation and of the world; a grand review of everything that goes to make life worth living passing in seemingly endless array before critical but bewildered humanity; an international exhibition of the resources and products of the earth and air, flood and field, established as one of the greatest "lions" of the metropolis.' Rather like Harrods today, Whiteley's was a 'sight' – as much an exhibition as a shop. Both impressive and unsettling, it was a clear demonstration that, for all but a select few, 50 or so years of attempts to control Victorian taste had largely failed.

63 Robe, 1895–1900. Made in the 'Artistic and Historic costume studio' of Liberty & Co., London, for a member of the Liberty family. The design was based on 16th-century gowns. Aesthetic sunflowers and pomegranates decorate the brocade; the colours are in the muted 'artistic' range of the 1890s. Silk and cotton brocade with a silk-satin front panel, silk-plush edgings and a taffeta lining. VAM T.57-1976.

65

186   PUNCH, OR THE LONDON CHARIVARI.   [OCTOBER 20, 1894.

FELICITOUS QUOTATIONS.

Hostess (of Upper Tooting, showing new house to Friend). "WE'RE VERY PROUD OF THIS ROOM, MRS. HOMINY. OUR OWN LITTLE UPHOLSTERER DID IT UP JUST AS YOU SEE IT, AND ALL OUR FRIENDS THINK IT WAS *LIBERTY!*"
Visitor (sotto voce). "'OH, LIBERTY, LIBERTY, HOW MANY CRIMES ARE COMMITTED IN THY NAME!'"

66

64 Armchair, 1899–1900. Designed by George Walton. Made for Liberty & Co. by William Birch of High Wycombe, Buckinghamshire. Walton, who began his career in Glasgow, moved to London in 1897, where he was one of a number of independent designers working for Liberty's, which also had its own design studio. Walnut, inlaid with mother-of-pearl. [h. 113.5cm]. VAM W.78-1975.

65 Whiteley's in Westbourne Grove, London, about 1900. A photograph taken at about 4.30 p.m., the fashionable shopping hour for the 'carriage trade'. The Hulton Getty Picture Collection.

66 The unhappy impact of Liberty's in the suburbs. Cartoon by George du Maurier in *Punch*, 20 October 1894. Wood engraving. VAM PP.8.L.

COMMERCIAL PROPAGANDA

Julia Bigham

During the Victorian period an increasing number of ready-made products – ranging from dress to furniture and food – became available to an expanding middle-class market. New types of advertising made the most of contemporaneous improvements in communications. New retailing strategies were devised, including larger shops, some of which had several different departments selling a variety of goods in ever more elaborate displays.

Many of the more radical and avant-garde shops such as Liberty's and Heal's were aimed at an élite market that led taste, yet they too turned to the relatively novel promotional tools of mail-order catalogues and, in the case of Heal's, nationwide press advertising.

The widespread use of pictorial advertising followed the introduction of cheaper methods

67. The 'Alne' brocaded satin. From *Liberty Catalogue No. 38*, 1896, published by Liberty & Co., London. Paper and boards. VAM NAL Liberty Catalogues.38.

of mass printing. Wood engraving and, later in the century, line-block etching were used to illustrate trade catalogues. Increasingly the illustrated press, including the *Illustrated London News* and *The Graphic*, featured advertisements with wood-engraved illustrations.

An important development was the widespread use of colour lithography in collectable magazine inserts and, most significantly,

posters. Typographical posters had covered hoardings and blank walls in British cities since the 1820s, but from the 1880s pictorial posters were increasingly in use. During the next decade these became more and more effective, following the rise of advertising agencies offering comprehensive advertising services, and of independent poster designers. At the same time more sophisticated packaging and branding were introduced for consumables. The most heavily advertised products, like Bovril and Colman's Mustard, became household names.

68. Advertisements from the *Illustrated London News*, 15 March 1884. VAM PP.10-1884.

69. Poster for Edwards' Desiccated Soup, about 1900. Created by the advertising agent S. H. Benson Ltd. Printed by Henry Blacklock & Co., Color Printers, Manchester. Colour lithograph. VAM E.33-1973.

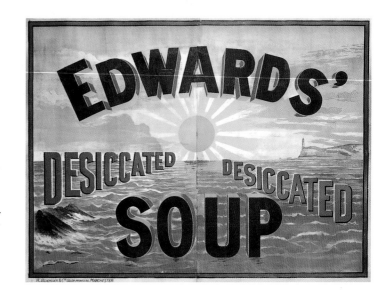

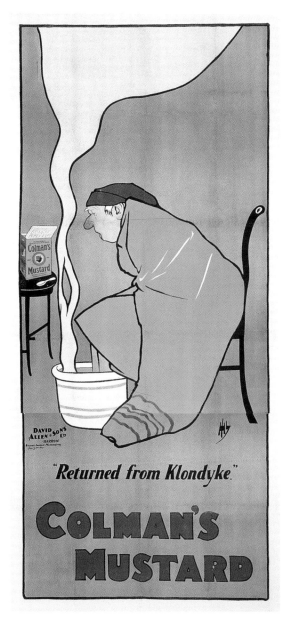

CHAPTER 4

Fashionable living

CHRISTOPHER BREWARD

1. The cult of domesticity

In 1847, just 10 years into the Victorian reign, the political author G. R. Porter noted the increased appearance of carpets in the homes of London shopkeepers. This was presented as proof of the rapid progress made by his compatriots in questions of taste and living standards since the end of the Georgian era. 'In the same houses,' he stated, 'we see not carpets merely, but many articles of furniture which were formerly found in use only among the nobility and gentry: the walls are covered with paintings and engravings, and the apartments contain evidences that some among the inmates cultivate one or more of those elegant accomplishments which tend so delightfully to refine the minds of individuals, and to sweeten the intercourse of families.' For Porter social, technological and material improvements went hand-in-hand, 'producing an increased amount of comfort to the great bulk of people'. Here was an affirmation of a growing national tendency to define moral and spiritual outlook through the choice of home decorations. Four years after Porter's observations, the Registrar-General George Graham could claim with some confidence, in his comments on the results of the 1851 Census, that 'the possession of an entire house is, it is true, strongly desired by every Englishman; for it throws a sharp, well-defined circle round his family and hearth – the shrine of his sorrows, joys, and meditations'.

The idea of the family home played a pivotal role in the organization of life across all levels of Victorian society. From its ordering of the social roles taken by men, women and children to its function as a statement of wealth and status, the private world of the household came to symbolize the distinctive and highly codified nature of nineteenth-century British civilization. In some ways the home was a contradictory space, proclaiming to the outside world the morals and tastes of its inhabitants in the most ostentatious manner, while providing behind the lace blinds of its windows a retreat from the 'vulgar'

2

world of paid labour and public discourse. Its interiors formed a setting for the proliferation of articles that marked the age as one of material excess. At the same time its walls and fences offered quasi-religious protection from the temptations that industrial and commercial life forced on a population increasingly dependent on the symbols of consumer culture as a way of making sense of things.

The concept of 'domesticity' allowed citizens to reconcile these tensions through an idealized way of life that was hierarchical and compartmentalized in the extreme. In the sphere of the home – whether this was located in the country mansion or West End palace of the aristocrat, the suburban villa of the middle classes or the model dwelling of the worker – every surface communicated carefully judged associations that attested to the worthiness of

---

1 Detail from *Evenings at Home*, 1852–3. By George Smith. The family of the administrator and design reformer Henry Cole gather in a room hung with the trophies of his career, protected from the cares of the outside world. Oil on canvas. Private collection.

2 *The Governess*, 1861. By Alice Squire. Even in a relatively humble setting the accoutrements of genteel living are displayed. Carpet, sprigged wallpaper, clean linen, framed prints and fresh flowers attest to the inhabitant's good character. Watercolour. The Geffrye Museum.

the inhabitants. Most especially they showed off the domestic talents of the lady of the house. The rhetoric of domesticity was clearly viewed as a feminine preserve. Men contributed to household concerns and benefited equally from their involvement in the creation of a domestic refuge, but its smooth running was the housewife's prerogative. At the apex of this system sat the family of the Queen, her ordered existence as wife, mother and head of state imposing a model on attempts by all other respectable people to do their duty as subjects,

through the proper management of their own homes. Such was the propaganda value of countless images of the first family at leisure in the gardens and state rooms of Windsor, Osborne and Balmoral that the powerful idea of homeliness could even be used to justify the management of a vastly expanding Empire. England itself became a 'home' across the seas to its imperial dominions and Victoria played the role of mother and, later in the century, grandmother to her colonized charges.

3

It is little wonder then, given its central position in the political and psychic formation of the state and its population, that the image of the Victorian home should retain such powerful associations. In its most stereotypical incarnation, the cluttered surfaces of its fireplaces and tabletops, the over-abundance of draperies and bibelots mark out the claustrophobic later-nineteenth-century household as the prime symbol of the epoch. Its mysterious depths and textured layers can be read now as a closely policed sanctuary of barely disguised neuroses and prejudices. They seem to capture all the most repressive aspects that have subsequently been associated with Victorian life. Yet it is important to remember that the interiors bound up with the cult of nineteenth-century domesticity also offered a stage set where even ordinary members of the population used the objects surrounding them to become new sorts of people and to behave in new ways, fashioning expressive new identities.

Domestic life was undoubtedly promoted as a rather restrictive ideal. Nevertheless beyond the front door other connected spheres of experience encouraged a release from the pressures of home and utilized public spaces as a further arena in which identities might be developed and even tested. A vigorous expansion of organized leisure activities outside the home, which witnessed a transformation in the worlds of shopping, travel excursions and evening entertainments, was justified by its relationship to the private aspirations of family life. Where the influence of the family ideal was absent – scorned at the edges of respectable society, or hidden among the slums of the very poor – alternative cultures fostered

3 *A Toxteth, Liverpool Drawing Room*, 1891. By H. Bedford Lemere. The architectural features of this middle-class drawing room in Liverpool are shrouded in the heavy drapes and trimmings associated with the worst excesses of Victorian decorating taste. The photographs and ornaments turn the mantelpiece into a family shrine.

spectacular forms of fashionable activity. These earned a glamorous sheen precisely because they stood in direct opposition to all that those more conservative notions of the domestic and the 'homely' suggested. The glitter of the demi-monde, which during the nineteenth century attached itself to everything from proletarian East End music hall to the courtesan's Mayfair salon, thus shimmered like a photographic negative, the reverse image of the cosy, but inward-looking spaces associated with the middle-class drawing room. Where these very different worlds were connected, and where both marked a development from the situation in previous periods, was in two areas. First, in the enthusiasm with which they embraced the commercial sphere and its products. Second, in their espousal of a fluid concept of 'lifestyle' as a means of negotiating a whole range of new and challenging social roles. Fashionable culture became the prime measure of where one stood in relation to society. People came to devote more hours than ever before to cultivating these fashionable concerns, both within the home and beyond it.

4 Photograph of an overpainted or retouched photograph of Queen Victoria and her family, 1857. Photographed by Caldesi and Montecchi. Albumen print. VAM 68:021.

5 *The Dancing Platform at Cremorne Gardens*, 1864. By Phoebus Levin. Cremorne was a popular pleasure garden in Chelsea, London, renowned as a meeting place for young men about town and women of loose morals. The vivid garments of the pleasure seekers identify them as inhabiting a world far removed from the safety of the respectable home. Oil on canvas. The Museum of London.

FURNISHING THE HOME

Laura Houliston

Home furnishing, always a priority for the Victorian middle classes, took on a new dynamism after the 1860s. The early Victorian middle-class interior owed much to its late-Georgian predecessor, but by the last 30 years of the nineteenth century there was far greater stylistic diversity.

In the nineteenth century most properties were rented. The artist Mary Ellen Best, daughter of a doctor, is known to have rented a house in York at the start of Victoria's reign and decorated it to her own taste. Possessions and decor in the drawing room were indicators to visiting guests of status, taste and wealth. Her drawing room has many recognizably 'Victorian' aspects, such as the chintz chair covers and buttoned upholstery, but it is strongly rooted in earlier Georgian styles, with features such as the outscrolled arms of the sofa and seat. In the 1850s and 1860s these

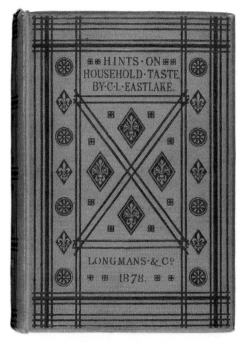

6. *Hints on Household Taste*, 1878. By Charles Eastlake. First published by Longmans & Co., 1868. VAM FW.6G10.

characteristic elements of early-Victorian drawing rooms were supplemented with newly fashionable furnishings, such as clocks in the French eighteenth-century style, polished carved tables, upright pianos, red turkey carpets and wallpaper with naturalistic patterns.

In the course of the Victorian period, reductions in manufacturing costs made a wider range of goods accessible to middle-class consumers. There were also improvements in services, with gas becoming commonplace in middle-class homes in the second half of the century. By 1890 this gave interiors a brightness not previously possible with oil lamps or candles. Shopping took on a new character from the middle of the century, with the spread of large department stores in the West End of London and elsewhere. Identifying, choosing and

7. *Our drawing room at York*, about 1838–40. By Mary Ellen Best. Watercolour. York City Art Gallery.

8. *The Chorale*, 1878. By John Atkinson Grimshaw, showing the artist's home in Scarborough, Yorkshire. Oil on canvas. Private collection.

9. Showcard for Henry Capel's Art Furniture, about 1875. Signed 'BB'. Printed by S. Straker & Sons, London. Photolithograph. VAM 29637:138.

purchasing household items usually involved the middle-class wife, as creative 'homemaker'. There were increasing numbers of specialist books, manuals and articles to give her advice, many of which came to advocate the new, 'artistic' manner of furnishing. Illustrated catalogues aimed at the middle-class consumer showed ranges of objects and interiors, at prices catering for different budgets. The choice available was staggering.

Under the influence of these developments, the furnishings of middle-class homes became increasingly diverse, with a mixture of styles and a proliferation of objects assembled from across the globe. The Scarborough house of the Yorkshire artist John Atkinson Grimshaw, as painted in 1878, juxtaposes eighteenth-century-style chairs, blue and white Chinese ceramic jars, Japanese fans and a Jacobean-style leaded window. Such juxtapositions were carried furthest in self-consciously 'artistic' interiors like Grimshaw's, but in the later years of the century many middle-class homes followed suit, with rooms full of objects in a variety of reproduction and 'artistic' styles.

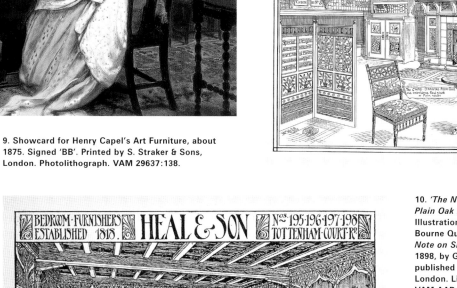

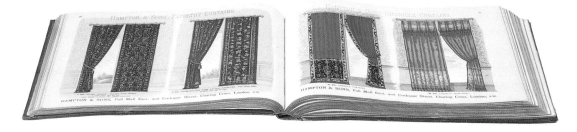

10. *'The Newlyn', A set of Plain Oak Furniture.* Illustration by Charles Henry Bourne Quennell, from A *Note on Simplicity of Design*, 1898, by Gleeson White, published by Heal & Son, London. Line-block. VAM AAD/1994/16/3251.

11. *Designs for Furniture and Decorations for Complete House Furnishings*, 1894. Catalogue for Hampton & Sons, London. VAM 505.C.44.

2. Planning the household

As far as the spatial organization of individual houses was concerned, the homes of the very wealthy – the landed rich, who maintained a social supremacy throughout most of the century – provided the stylistic model by which those of lower rank and income might gain an approximation of genteel living as complex as income and space would allow. At the time of the Queen's accession in 1837 roughly 3,000 large working country houses attached to significant estates stood as testament to the enduring political and economic power of landed families in Britain. It is thanks largely to the seriousness with which Victorian landowners took their duties as custodians of these piles that so many have survived virtually intact into the twenty-first century. Consideration for more modern styles of living, in the form of water closets, bathrooms, central heating, gas lighting, hydraulic lifts and mechanized kitchen equipment, was constrained by the unforgiving structures of older buildings

12

and, after 1870, by the cash drain represented by the huge swathes of land that generally came with them. Such luxuries could be accommodated only in the building of new country houses, of which about 500 were erected (including some remodelling of earlier structures) between 1835 and 1889. Half of these schemes were initiated by families profiting from relatively recent incomes raised through commerce and industry. Such patrons could only hope to emulate the far-reaching cultural clout of their landed neighbours. Nevertheless, their massive new mansions with all modern conveniences displayed an extraordinary level of comfort and fairly radical new ideas about polite living. They were revolutionary – but in the most discreet manner.

12 *The Last Day in the Old Home*, 1862. By Robert Braithwaite Martineau. The circumstances of modern life often placed landed families in a precarious financial position. Here the high living of a young aristocrat has forced the sale of his old country home and treasured heirlooms. Oil on canvas. © Tate, London, 2003.

13 The Drawing Room, Cragside, Northumberland. Designed by Norman Shaw. Built 1869–84 for the arms manufacturer, Sir William Armstrong. While the imposing neo-Mannerist fireplace, fine panelling and vaulted ceiling recall the traditional country house, upholstered furniture and modern light fittings provide the latest in comfortable living.

14 Ground-floor plan, Bear Wood, Berkshire. The spatial organization of the new country house was a feat of social engineering and rational planning. Rooms were identified according to the sex of their users.

13

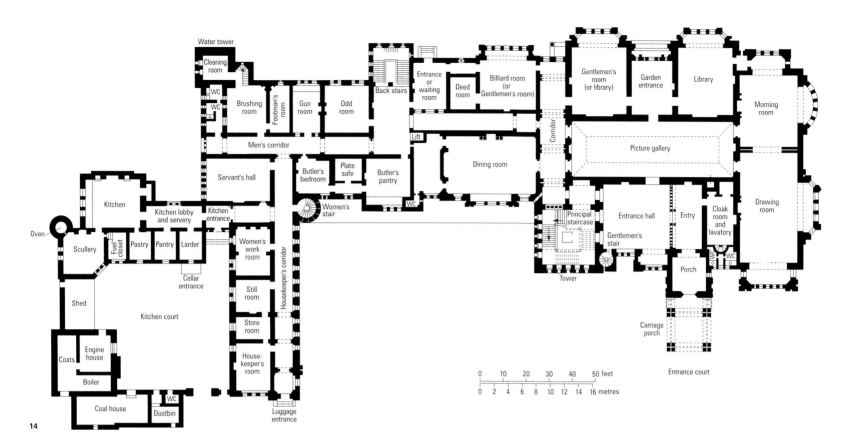

It was through this combination of deference to the old established order, whose arcane social rituals acted as a barrier against presumptuous incomers, and an openness to the lessons of modernity that the Victorian country house maintained its primacy as a model for 'correct' domestic arrangements. Many of these arrangements seemed to have common ground with more 'middle-class' notions of decency and propriety. Several of the organizational changes that took place were structural, relating to the spatial relationship of public and private, formal and informal areas. In most houses servants' wings were considerably expanded to support the role of the house as a centre for hospitality and entertainment. Serving staff and younger members of the family were moved out from the attic storeys to self-contained annexes, which also often included provision for nurseries and children's bedrooms. Here, though better provided for, they were also removed from polite eyes. The more socially homogeneous set-up of the eighteenth-century aristocratic household gave way to a class consciousness which dictated that in some houses servants turn to face the wall in the unexpected presence of family members. Children – though an essential component of the family atmosphere that formed a focus of household activities – were similarly side-lined wherever possible until they were old enough for despatch to public school or the care of a governess.

15 *Bear Wood, Berkshire*, 1870. From *The Architect*, 9 July 1870. Drawing by Robert Kerr, lithograph by Kell Bros. Bear Wood was completed in 1870 to designs by Kerr for the newspaper proprietor John Walter. Lithograph. VAM PP.21.D.

This strict segregation of activities and social types was even echoed in the treatment of guests, who found their sleeping quarters diminished in size and separated into men's and women's wings. Old-style private dressing and receiving rooms were largely discarded in favour of communal morning, drawing, garden, music, smoking, reading and billiard rooms where everyone might congregate at specific times of the day. These were also clearly divided according to use, so that the final three rooms retained overtly masculine associations. Any taint of rakish licentiousness was swept away in preference for moral and architectural control. At the centre of the house the family reinforced its symbolic prominence through a revival of the medieval hall. This served as the focus for public events: everything from society balls to servants' dances, from dinners for tenant farmers to parties for local school children. In this sentimental vein the great English country house and its mistress maintained their hold on the popular imagining of English cultural and social life well into the twentieth century, even as the inevitable demise of this way of living was being loudly trumpeted.

These clearly demarcated boundaries whereby the layout of the building reflected the morality of its inhabitants were replicated on a smaller scale in the town houses of the rich, and especially in the suburban dwellings of the middle classes. Similar effects could be discerned in the arrangement of the 'parlour' of the 'respectable' working classes, where the best room of the house

17

was set aside as a well-tidied shrine, filled with mementoes of family life, prized ornaments, religious ephemera and patriotic memorabilia. By the last quarter of the century many parlours incorporated a piano, the ultimate proof of respectability and a sign of Sunday-evening sociability. Indeed, it is arguable that the refined territories of new lifestyles – aristocratic, middle-class and proletarian – signalled an almost universal acceptance of the morally earnest codes of social behaviour associated with evangelical Christianity. The daughter of a Hertfordshire vicar, recalling a move to a new parish in 1847, presented a description of home life whose abstract considerations were not so far removed from those that might also concern the daughter of a duke or a dustman:

> The house contained a tiled entrance lobby and oak-floored hall, dining room, drawing room and study, three best bedrooms and two dressing rooms, two servants' rooms and two nurseries. These latter were in a wing approached by a baize-covered swing door, and back stairs led down to the kitchen, pantry and a small parish room . . . there were no bathrooms then, and all hot and cold water had to be carried from the kitchen and scullery. But we all had baths each day in spite of that. Oil lamps and candles were used for lighting. Our drawing room was papered with a buff and gilt Fleurs-de-Lys patterned paper. There were book shelves and pier glasses and wool-work ottomans and an upright grand piano with faded red silk fluted across the front and a very fine harp . . . The carpet was red with a buff pattern, and my mother had a davenport sacred to her own use. In the best bedrooms there were four-post beds with damask curtains, though brass beds were by then becoming fashionable . . . Our household consisted of a cook, house parlour maid and a girl.

16

16 *Design for the Great Hall at Scarisbrick Hall, Lancashire*, 1836. By A. W. N. Pugin. Scarisbrick was remodelled for its rich 19th-century inheritors. The Great Hall was a symbolic focus for the household. Water-colour. RIBA Library Drawings Collection.

17 *Interior of a Cottage at Compton Bassett, Wiltshire*, 1849. By Elizabeth Pearson Dalby. The array of humble possessions reinforces an impression of worthy homeliness. Gouache. © Salisbury and South Wiltshire Museum.

18 *View of a Living Room*, 1909. By C. W. Bodman. By the turn of the century the middle- and working-class parlour had become a show room for inherited furniture and the pursuance of 'respectable' hobbies, including music making, embroidery, flower arranging and painting. Such was the emotional importance of its content that its use was often restricted to Sundays and holidays. Watercolour, pen and ink. VAM E.1273-1984.

19 *Playing at Doctors*, 1863. By Frederick Daniel Hardy. Though slightly frayed at the edges, the interiors of the houses belonging to country vicars and doctors had become a familiar symbol of the 'cosy' middle-class lifestyle by mid-century. Oil on canvas. VAM 1035-1886.

20

Closer in to the rapidly expanding cities, suburban developments of detached, semi-detached and terraced villas followed similar ground-plans, their occupants striving for the same effects, even as space and financial means declined. The trappings of gentility were still in evidence in the jerry-built ribbons of two- and three-storey, narrow and rather dark houses with their italianate or Gothic embellishments, which ringed every sizeable town in Britain by the 1870s.

From the city centre outwards the class hierarchies of Victorian society could be read through the rental value, garden length and room size of a home. Meanwhile the decorative details of mass-produced ornamental brick and stone work, stucco, stained glass and coloured roof tiles on the exterior, and of moulded plaster cornices, volutes and ceiling roses, cast-iron fireplaces, baths and kitchen ranges on the interior, remained constant across a highly variegated social spectrum.

20 *Builders in Clapton Passage, Hackney, London*, 1882. By Alfred Braddock. Nestled between older 18th-century developments and boasting decorative embellishments drawn from a mixture of classical and Gothic sources, the terraced house, constructed by local builders as a speculation, incorporated all the aspirations of a new generation of suburban inhabitants. London Borough of Hackney, Archives Department.

21

Such markers of distinction differed perhaps only in quality and quantity according to the spending power of the respective speculative builder, but some form of elaboration was always present. Thus poorer clerks, schoolteachers, small traders and their families struggled at the inner perimeters to define themselves against the perceived roughness of their working-class neighbours. Professionals in law and medicine, or those whose retail and service businesses guaranteed a substantial income without the need to commute, inhabited larger outlying properties whose grounds had been carved out from the sale of old estates and whose street patterns followed the lanes of ancient villages that had been swallowed up by the urban sprawl. Standing between the successful lawyers and the minor gentry were those stockbrokers and industrial entrepreneurs who peppered the rural hinterlands of urban centres with extravagant domestic edifices that testified to old values and new technologies.

21 *Silver Moonlight*, 1886. By John Atkinson Grimshaw. At the edge of the city, old and new houses in spacious grounds served the domestic needs of urban professionals. Grimshaw delighted in producing composite landscapes based on the prosperous suburbs of northern industrial towns, where crumbling mansions and winding village lanes suggested a more romantic and picturesque conception of modern life. Oil on canvas. Harrogate Museums and Art Gallery.

In between all of these building projects lay the results of earlier booms, and it would be wrong to assume that all Victorians lived in new properties. However, most interiors could be updated to incorporate modern ideas of comfort and hygiene. In 1881 the architect Robert Edis provided encouragement for owners of outmoded Georgian terraces. In his book *The Decoration and Furniture of Town Houses* he suggested that stairwells be brightened with framed drawings, china, leaded lantern lights, flower arrangements and Persian prayer carpets. Dining rooms should be 'designed for use, not show', with well-sprung chairs 'covered with strong, serviceable

leather . . . in preference to velvet, which is liable to hold dust and to drag the lace of ladies' dresses'. Cumbersome sideboards might be replaced with 'a plain but solidly handsome buffet, arranged for the reception of plate and glass, or for good pieces of china'. In accordance with common practice, 'drawing rooms should be the rooms of all others in which good taste . . . should be everywhere apparent'. This meant discarding 'dreary blanks of mere one-tinted paper' for wall displays of 'pleasant objects to look upon' and 'comfortable couches and chairs to lounge and really rest upon'. The mid-century fashion for 'fluffy wool mats . . . antimacassars of lace . . . [and] bits of Dresden' was to

22 *The drawing room, 3 The Close, Winchester*, about 1900. By B. O. Corfe. The drawing room in the house of Canon A. S. Valpy. During the last quarter of the century the sensitive and 'artistic' homemaker pared down the formal heaviness of previous decades for a lighter touch in which the informality of chintz covers, random piles of books and fine antique furniture betrayed 'superior' taste and learning. Watercolour. VAM E.222-1955.

"YES MOTHER, I COME! I COME!"

23

be pared back so that 'the rooms should, above all, look and be home-like in all their arrangements, with ornaments, books and flowers, not arranged merely for show, but for pleasant study or recreation'. Considerations of health dictated the refitting of bedrooms, which 'should be clear of everything that can collect and hold dust in any form'. Light, simple furniture, including tiled wash-stands, portable dressing tables and deal window seats, together with an avoidance of densely patterned surfaces that 'might be likely to fix themselves upon the tired brain' lent an airiness to cramped attic spaces. Adjoining nurseries could be modernized with flower boxes, washable wallpapers and pasted borders utilizing the colourful Christmas book illustrations of 'Miss Kate Greenaway and Mr Walter Crane'.

24

23 Poster for the play *East Lynne*, about 1895. By an unknown artist. The Victorian house demanded intensive maintenance, and an interest in issues of health dictated that washable and accessible surfaces were introduced, especially in bedrooms such as this, with its iron bed. Lithograph. VAM E.166-1935.

24 *Winter*, 1883. Tile. Designed by Kate Greenaway. Made by T. and R. Boote. Glazed earthenware. VAM Circ.398-1962.

So what distinguished the Victorian period was the relative ease with which middle-class occupants could move between property types and impose their character on empty spaces in the manner that Edis advised. This was a luxury previously reserved for the very rich, or a necessity imposed on the transient poor. Despite the seeming clutter of domestic arrangements, the popularity of renting property over its outright purchase made for a surprisingly mobile urban population, which must have impacted on the increasing turnover and emphasis on portability in styles of furnishing and decoration. Those who bought their own houses were either unusually wealthy or, in the case of the aggressively self-made, déclassé, which led to accusations of fanciful tawdriness against those who used their dwellings as a direct illustration of their wealth (the *arriviste* family with its vulgar tastes was a constant target for satirists like Dickens).

The landlord system ensured that overtly individualized expressions of capital accumulation were kept in check, on the outside of buildings at least. 'Good taste' was more profitably displayed through regular removals to the latest suburban development ('regular' meaning that the middle classes typically took on renewable leases of one to three years, while working-class

26

tenancies were agreed by the week or month). The constant erection of new streets in the latter half of the nineteenth century offered the house-hunter a range of ready-made external finishes in neo-classical, Gothic and vernacular styles, in districts attuned to minute social gradations that might correspond to shared occupations, religious affiliations, fashionable pretensions or even political sympathies. The freedom of renting also meant that accommodation could be tailored according to stages of the lifecycle, with more or fewer rooms taken on as the family unit expanded and contracted. Furthermore, with an average of only 10 per cent of income given over to the landlord, relatively prosperous Victorians could devote a large proportion of their wealth to other priorities, which included the funding of businesses, the hiring of servants and the education of dependants. This extra money also (and most importantly) went towards the purchase of clothing and furnishings whose opulent surfaces provided a key index of status.

---

25 *An Ordinary Mantlepiece*, 1878. Illustration from *The Drawing Room; Its Decorations and Furniture* by Lucy Orrinsmith, 1878. While the permanent fittings of rented Victorian houses were often heavy and bulky, new tenants could do much to impose their character on their surroundings with the judicious introduction of ornaments and textiles. Wood engraving. VAM 47.D.38.

3. Accounting for taste

These circumstances both gave rise to an unprecedented multiplication in the number and type of objects on the market. They also opened the floodgates for a deluge of publications that claimed to guide the consumer through an increasingly fraught voyage of self-construction. It seems fair, therefore, to claim that the Victorians – though they would not have recognized the word in its modern sense – were the first generation to succumb to the idea of 'lifestyle'. As the opinions of design reformers and the innovations of producers and retailers impacted on the appearance and use of a proliferation of new objects, this apparent freedom of choice evolved into a highly nuanced value system, whereby the dual influences of morality and fashion dictated that what you purchased really signified who you were. From the 1860s onwards this was true in all spheres of domestic life, from the laying of the dinner table, through the arrangement of pictures on the wall to your choice of wardrobe content. What, when and where you bought, and how you put it to use, said as much about you as the background of your parents or the way you earned your living – and sometimes more. Of course, to an extent this had always been the case, but now, as the pool of consumers widened and diversified, the manufacturers and purveyors of luxury and fashionable goods were far more efficient in ensuring that their products conveyed the appropriate social and cultural messages – messages that were deliberately prone to the vagaries of shifting styles, social habits and 'fads'.

26 *The Awakening Conscience*, 1853. By William Holman Hunt. Every surface of this interior has been chosen by the artist to symbolize the shallow material trappings of a 'kept' woman in her St John's Wood, London, boudoir. Oil on canvas. © Tate, London, 2003.

27 *For Sale*, 1857. By James Collinson. This young woman appears to be the epitome of respectable femininity, fulfilling her charitable duties at a church bazaar. But it is not immediately clear whether it is the table of attractive wares or the woman herself that is for sale. Oil on canvas. Castle Museum and Art Gallery, Nottingham.

28 *Changing Homes*, 1862. By George Elgar Hicks. Not all acquisition was necessarily corrupting. Hicks depicts a proud array of glittering wedding gifts and strikingly coloured upholstery and dress textiles in the comfortable drawing room of an affluent London family. Oil on canvas. The Geffrye Museum.

THE DINING TABLE

Ann Eatwell

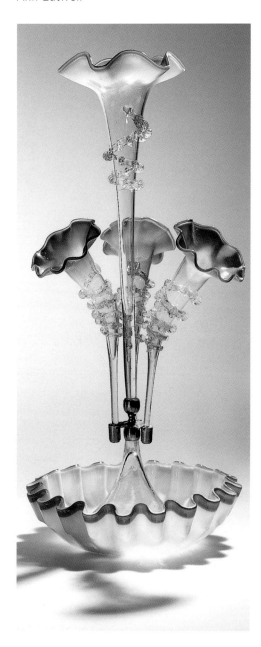

The high-Victorian dining table looked very different from that of the Georgian period. The change was prompted by a new method of serving dinner known as *à la russe*, which replaced the earlier service *à la française*. Jane Carlyle (wife of the Scottish writer Thomas Carlyle) describes dining *à la russe* with the novelist Charles Dickens in 1849. 'The dinner was served up in the new fashion – not placed on the table at all – but handed round (by servants) – only the dessert on the table and quantities of artificial flowers.' Inherited silver was replaced by modern glass and ceramics, and on tables set *à la russe* the place setting or cover assumed greater importance. Despite a reluctance to abandon the old style of dining – public debate on the issue even reached the letter pages of *The Times* – by the 1860s polite society had largely embraced the new method of service.

The dinner party was the centrepiece of Victorian social entertaining, especially during the London season, which followed the parliamentary session from April to July. Celebrities were in great demand at such dinners. By June 1879 the author Henry James claimed to have dined out 107 times after the success of his

31. *Dinner at Haddo House*, 1884. By Alfred Edward Emslie. The man in the centre talking to the hostess is Mr Gladstone, the Prime Minister. Oil on canvas. National Portrait Gallery, London.

29. Centrepiece, 1890–1900. Possibly made at Stourbridge, West Midlands. Glass and brass. [h. 54.4cm]. VAM Circ.193-1970.

30. Specialist utensils. From left to right: fish knife and fork, with hallmarks for 1902–3. Silver with mother-of-pearl handles. Butter knife, about 1890. Electroplated nickel silver. Asparagus tongs, about 1890. Electroplated nickel silver. Lobster pick. Electroplated nickel silver. Cheese scoop, with London hallmarks for 1894–5. Silver with ivory handle. Grape scissors, late 19th century. Electroplated nickel silver. VAM Circ.102-1953, M.27A-1967, loan: NRM York.1:12-1999, M.26-2000, M.24-1999, M.41-2000.

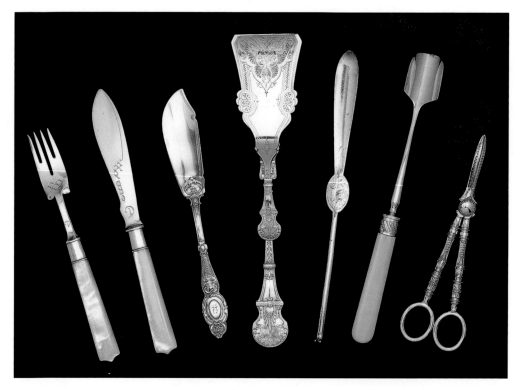

34. Breakfast, hash and soup serving dish with revolving cover, about 1905. Made in Sheffield by Aitkin Brothers. Presented to Captain Frank Johnson by the officers of HM Prison, Pentonville, on his retirement on 2 December 1905. Electroplated nickel silver. VAM M.28-2000.

novel *Daisy Miller*. Many society dinners were reciprocal affairs, described as 'cutlet for cutlet', at which hospitality was returned. Giving a dinner was the middle-class housewife's contribution to upward social mobility, for a successful dinner could advance her husband's career. It required careful planning of the menu, guest list, table setting and serving of dishes by permanent or hired staff.

Domestic management manuals, such as Mrs Beeton's *Book of Household Management* advised on every aspect of organizing the dinner party, from seasonal menus for serving *à la russe* or *à la française* to the choice of dining equipment and layout of the table

itself. Numerous etiquette books enabled the inexperienced or those with new money to move in good company. Dining etiquette formed an important part of the Victorian code of polite society. *The Manners and Rules of Good Society* (1879) focused on the complicated and changing use of cutlery. With a few exceptions, like eating bread and some kinds of fruit, touching food with the fingers was frowned upon. Diners were presented with a growing – and sometimes confusing – range of specialist utensils for eating particular foods. It was important to be able to recognize lobster picks, asparagus tongs and grape scissors, and to know how to use them correctly.

32. Place setting for dinner, set out according to Mrs Beeton's *Book of Household Management*, 1888. Silver flatware, with hallmarks for 1893–1904. From the outside: table spoon, fish knife, fish fork, knife and fork for first course, knife and fork for main course. Salt cellars, with London hallmarks for 1874–5. Silver and enamel. Glassware, from left to right: comport, about 1864. Swan flower trough, 1870–1900. Champagne, sherry and wine glasses, about 1880–90. VAM M.33-39-2000, M.29-1983, Circ.748-1967, C.270-1987, C.37-2000, C.40-2000, C.36-2000.

33. A dining table. Illustration from *The Book of Household Management* by Isabella Beeton, 1888. Coloured wood engraving. Private collection.

35

In the domestic sphere the effects of expanded consumer options can be traced through an incursion of fashionable styling into home decoration, which reached its peak by the 1880s. Each room in the house could be fitted out through reference to a battery of decorating styles, plundered from historical and global sources to create a virtual index to the aesthetic knowhow of the householder and the traditional function of the space in question. As early as 1865 the journal *London Society* could elaborate on 'seven styles of furniture' that summarized (in a satirical vein) the spectrum of cosmopolitan tastes. The 'dull' style approximated to the traditional manner of decorating the drawing room since the 1840s and symbolized home as a comforting retreat from the world of fashion: 'neatness . . . highly polished round table . . . wax flowers under a glass shade . . . a bit of needlework . . . well-bound books'. The writer of the piece felt that 'one never goes into the room without feeling inclined to yawn, and a sense of depression comes over

36

35 *Past and Present No. 1*, 1858. By Augustus Egg. Behind the respectable 'dullness' of the mid-century drawing room all manner of emotional problems might be hidden. This interior has been carefully put together to suggest the fragility of the domestic ideal. In its formal details it shows the prevailing middle-brow taste for dark reds and greens and is perhaps less cluttered than clichéd representations of middle-class rooms might have led us to expect. Oil on canvas. © Tate, London, 2003.

36 *Hush! (The Concert)*, about 1875. By James Tissot. The huge public rooms of great London houses provided the grandiose settings for those formal receptions that marked the social season. Attendance at such events in the correct attire was proof of acceptance into the world of the social élite. Oil on canvas. Manchester City Art Gallery.

one in a few minutes'. The 'upholsterer's' style lacked emotional authenticity and was condemned for its adherence to pattern books. 'The upholsterer goes down with rule and tape . . . and he stamps himself and his shop upon the whole house . . . The drawing room must be white and gold; the dining room red and mahogany; and the library oak and leather.' The 'rich' style took such attitudes to extremes. The author bemoaned that 'heavy massive wealth overpowers it all', and in images of élite interiors, complex draperies, massed reproduction furniture and gilt stucco give some indication of the prevalence of this trend, especially in the cavernous saloons that provided space for the society balls that punctuated the 'season'. In the 1850s and 1860s the 'architectural' style alluded to the taste for all things Gothic. *London Society* associated its use with the furnishing of bedrooms. 'When we saw it we thanked heaven we were not going to sleep in those beds. Imagine the horrors of a nightmare of griffins impaled, or lions rampant, or the ceaselessness of the motto from which one could never escape.' Certainly the ingenious forms of medieval decoration were utilized to disguise objects of more mundane usage, including the technology of bathrooms, water closets and kitchens. The 'antiquarian' style, with its dark panelling and uncomfortable settee 'in which it was supposed some great man had sat a century or two ago', clearly found favour in masculine studies and libraries, while the 'luxurious' and 'meretricious' styles in their sybaritic whimsy came closest to a fusion of the upholsterer's and the couturier's art. In their theatrical showiness, such interiors paid a debt to the new public spaces of hotels, town halls and places of entertainment – the antithesis of the highly personalized and shrine-like inner-sanctum of the drawing room:

> This style abounds in white and gold, and beautifully tinted walls half darkened by rose-coloured blinds, and surrounded by balconies filled with evergreens and bright flowers, and ornamented with arches of creepers . . . there is a great amount of looking glass; a profusion of drapery in the shape of portieres and curtains. The effect is pretty, but it is all more or less a sham . . . It is pretentious, and attempts to pass itself off for something that it is not.

37 The guest bedroom in the Tower House, Kensington, London, 1885. From *The House of William Burges* by Richard Popplewell Pullan. Photograph. VAM 51.E.54.

38 The Drawing Room, 34 Grosvenor Square, London, 1890. By H. Bedford Lemere. By the end of the century élite interiors were increasingly being styled with sweeping draperies and trimmings, lush vegetation and neo-rococo furniture, which made it difficult to distinguish the interiors of a fashionable hotel from a private drawing room. Indeed, both were theatrical spaces that permitted a conscious display of fashionability by society women. Albumen print. VAM 186-1926.

39

white china, Japanese paper fans, lacquered screens and all the paraphernalia of the 'artistic' sensibility. In the same year that *The Magazine of Art* was encouraging a rejection of the merely fashionable, Mrs Orrinsmith of Beckenham in her book for middle-class housewives, *The Drawing Room; its decoration and furniture*, was showing readers how to negotiate the blurred boundaries between aestheticism and consumerism:

> To an appreciative mind, not spoiled by the luxury of wealth, what keen pleasure there is in the possession of one new treasure; a Persian tile, an Algerian flower-pot, an old Flemish cup, a piece of Nankin blue . . . not one being costly, yet each in its own way, beautiful and interesting . . . A delight as pure as that of a child with a fresh toy, and superior to that in its lasting power, is open to the aspirant after the beautiful in art.

By the 1880s this striving for pretty effects had precipitated the first popular interior-decorating craze, whereby all pretence at creating a moral refuge from the world had become bound up with a desire to express individuality of spirit through the purchase of objects. In the guise of the aesthetic movement, fashion finally made a successful assault on the citadel of middle-class respectability. In its early stages the trend carried traces of moral didacticism through its close association with the political philosophies of Arts and Crafts pioneers like William Morris and Walter Crane. Its proselytizers recommended that the confident individuality expressed in their own bohemian interiors and the discretion to choose honest, well-made artefacts should be enough to construct a pleasing and meaningful environment. In 1878 a correspondent for *The Magazine of Art* urged readers to trust their own instincts: 'If you like white walls have white walls, although your neighbours prefer blue walls, and if you like dark walls don't be afraid of having them, because you hear that a drawing-room should be furnished in the French style.' Such breezy optimism was severely constrained in a world where manufacturers, retailers and publishers were increasingly adept at riding the market. The taste for constructing fantastic settings that played on the imagination was swiftly answered by the commercial provision of blue and

40

---

39 *The Dining Room at The Grange, North End Road*, 1898. By Thomas Matthews Rooke. The 'artistic' interior (this one belonging to the painter Edward Burne-Jones in Fulham, London) was at first intended as the antithesis of the fashionable 'decorator's' room. Its self-conscious display of personal treasures promotes the exotic and the quaint over the mass-produced or received notions of good taste. Watercolour. Private collection.

40 *My Aesthetic Love*, 1881. Music cover by Alfred Concanen. By the 1880s the paraphernalia of 'aesthetic' taste was widely available to a broad metropolitan audience. The pretensions of the craze's followers were cruelly lampooned by satirists. Colour lithograph. VAM Enthoven Collection.

41

THE FASHIONS

Expressly designed and prepared for the

Englishwoman's Domestic Magazine.

JULY 1860

42

4. Providing for desires

The commercial success of the aesthetic movement can be attributed to a number of factors. The circulation of definitions and instructions in popular magazines, the promotion of emblems through advertising and other forms of popular culture, and the provision of products in the retail sphere ensured that the trend was brought right into the homes of even the proudly unsophisticated (such as the fictional Mr Pooter of Holloway, London, in the Grossmiths' *Diary of a Nobody*). Mass-market journalism, advertisements and attractively stocked shops were not new phenomena. The important innovations in these industries had been initiated in the eighteenth century. What had changed was the scale and efficiency of their production, and nowhere were the effects more keenly felt than in activities surrounding the acquisition and use of fashionable dress.

For both middle- and upper-class Victorian women, fashion in clothing was on the surface a phenomenon that was firmly associated with Paris, which had long been established as a centre for the luxury trades. In the magazines that provided monthly and later weekly information on the progression of sartorial taste, editors always deferred to the styles being worn in France, and the intricate coloured fashion-plates that accompanied women's journals were generally produced by French publishing companies. However, this Gallic façade disguised an attitude to dressing up that was as closely attuned to British concerns with social differentiation and gentility as the decoration of the home. Periodicals themselves (of which many were launched over the course of the period) were carefully oriented towards the needs of specific classes of readers.

STYLISH OUTDOOR COSTUMES, DESIGNED AT THE MAISON WORTH, PARIS. 43

Thus *The Englishwoman's Domestic Magazine*, edited by Samuel and Isabella Beeton, enjoyed a heyday in the 1850s and 1860s as the 'style bible' of middle-class women, each edition being eagerly awaited for its even-tempered advice on the trappings of polite society and its increasingly racy correspondence pages. Its successor, *Myra's Journal of Dress and Fashion*, which dominated the 1870s and 1880s, aimed its content at a broader readership, encouraging those of more straitened financial means to adapt and modernize their wardrobes with the aid of practical patterns and dressmaking tips. Titles such as *The Queen* and *The Season* confined their columns to the concerns of the 'Upper Ten', those aristocratic and plutocratic readers who sought guidance on appropriate wear for fashionable society events and were able to enjoy, and even purchase, the Paris gowns by couturiers like Worth or Doucet that featured in the magazines' pages.

---

41 *He is Dead Too*, about 1888. By Walter Weedon Grossmith. Drawing for an illustration in *The Diary of a Nobody* by George and Weedon Grossmith, 1892. Japanese fans appear even on the walls of the Grossmiths' fictional clerk in unfashionable suburban London. Pen and ink drawing. VAM E.634-1987.

42 *The Fashions. Expressly designed and prepared for the Englishwoman's Domestic Magazine*, July 1860. By Jules David. Engraved and printed in Paris by J. Fourmage. Images of French fashions were made available to the middle-class readership of English women's magazines. Hand-coloured engraving. VAM PP.19.F.

43 *Stylish Outdoor Costumes, designed at the Maison Worth, Paris*, 1895. By Adolphe Charles Sandoz, engraved in Paris by Derbier. From *The Queen. The Lady's Newspaper*, August 1895. For the wealthy reader magazines promoted the creations of Paris designers, including Charles Worth. Engraving. VAM PP.7.C.

44

45

'Parisian' was also an epithet used by British purveyors of fashionable goods. Corsetiers, milliners and dressmakers, from the élite traders of Bond Street to the back-street concerns of Bolton, all deferred to the superiority of French associations in their promotions. Yet the textile and wholesale industries of Manchester, Glasgow and London benefited from a massive boom during the Victorian period, and the goods they offered carried definite British characteristics at home and in the Empire. In her actual purchases the British consumer was resolutely patriotic. The idea of Paris was really little more than a marketing tool and its broader cultural connotations were in any case rather disreputable! Thus the reasonably fashionable middle-class Englishwoman called on a wide range of local outlets to service her clothing needs over the course of the nineteenth century. Small family drapery and outfitting shops, little changed since the Napoleonic Wars, provided a range of suitable fabrics, accessories, underwear and ready-made items, while the skills of private seamstresses could convert the fantasies of fashion-plates into a more constrained reality. For the richer client a wide range of court dressmakers in the West End were more than capable of producing the elaborately constructed confections of silk, lace and velvet necessary for presentation ceremonies at St James's Palace or the round of 'at homes', musical soirées, fancy-dress parties, dinners and formal balls that constituted the social season.

---

44 *Colworth House, Bedfordshire,*
1850. By Eugène Louis Lami.
Expensively dressed guests socialize
at a Bedfordshire country house.
Watercolour. VAM 169-1880.

45 *Horatio Sparkins,* about 1836. Illustration by George
Cruikshank for *Sketches by Boz* by Charles Dickens, 1836.
The creation of a fashionable wardrobe still depended to a
large degree on the expertise of a range of small traders,
including the draper (seen here) and the dressmaker.
Etching. VAM 9726.6.

The newer city-centre department stores, which had developed from shawl and mantle warehouses in the 1830s and 1840s, probably accounted for a fairly small proportion of the typical consumer's purchases. Nevertheless, their impact on the urban scene and on the practice of shopping was hugely significant. With their spectacular window displays and interior fittings, their guarantee of fixed prices and dependable quality, and their provision of such luxuries as tea rooms, resident orchestras and armies of accommodating staff, London stores such as Peter Robinson in Oxford Street, Harrods in Brompton Road, Whiteley's in Bayswater and Liberty in Regent Street became leviathans of the high street – each appealing to its own constituency of consumers. Improvements in public transport systems ensured that regular trips into town became a crucial social and familial duty for the diligent housewife or hostess. By the 1890s this transformation of metropolitan life and the sense of urban excitement that it engendered had been bolstered by the opening of

46 *The Bayswater Omnibus*, about 1895. By George William Joy. Shopping for fashionable goods entailed a direct engagement with the noise, visual distractions and social variety of modern urban life. Reliable public transport offered the commercial experience of the metropolis to a growing audience. Oil on canvas. The Museum of London.

47 Oxford Street, London, 1896.

THE RAILWAYS

Jim Cheshire

The Railway Station was one of the most popular paintings of the Victorian period. Its popularity reflected the public's fascination with its subject matter. The *Telegraph* eulogized 'that microcosm of our life journey, the railway platform', while for the *Illustrated London News* the railways represented 'the grandest exponent of the enterprise, the wealth and the intelligence of our race'. Few disputed the central position that the railways held in Victorian culture.

Unlike their European counterparts, British railways were built with private money. The companies formed to finance their construction became enormously powerful through the huge amount of capital invested in them. They were unique in that they had no traditions to conform to. They represented themselves to the public in innovative ways: issuing their staff with fine uniforms, painting carriages and locomotives in distinctive colour schemes and adopting heraldic motifs.

Railway companies used buildings as well as uniforms to create a corporate identity. George Gilbert Scott's great Gothic building at St Pancras announced that the Midland Railway

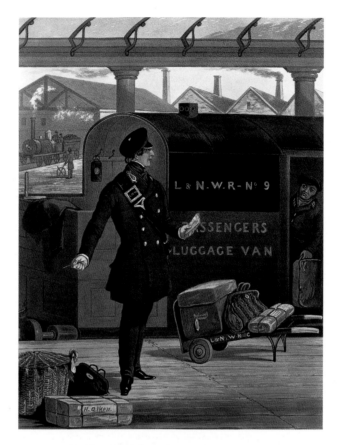

48. *The Guard of 1852*. By J. Harris after Samuel Henry Alken. Aquatint. Corporation of London.

49. *Travelling on the Liverpool and Manchester Railway, 1833*. By John Byam Liston Shaw. Aquatint. Chartered Institute of Transport.

had its own line between London and Yorkshire. It dwarfed the nearby Great Northern Hotel and King's Cross station, the property of the Great Northern Railway company. Fitting out the hotel at St Pancras provided valuable contracts for art manufacturers; Gillows, Elkington, Skidmore and Osler all profited from major contracts.

The Victorian railways provided a conspicuous physical manifestation of Britain's class structure: first-, second- and third-class carriages demarcated degrees of wealth and social standing. 'Parliamentary' trains – introduced after government legislation in 1844 – provided cheap travel for the lower classes, but could be slow and uncomfortable. Nevertheless, by the last quarter of the century the politician John Bright could point out that, although the railway network had increased the power of the rich, 'it has given to the poor a power which they did not at all possess'.

Increased mobility provided new opportunities for work and leisure. Daily commuting now became a possibility, while daytrips and weekend breaks became features of many people's lives. 'Excursion' trains

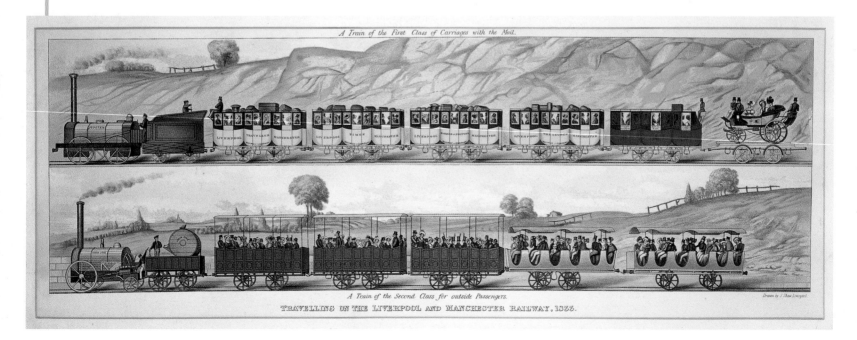

50. *Design for the south elevation of the Grand Midland Hotel, St Pancras Station, London*, about 1865. By Sir George Gilbert Scott. Pen and wash. RIBA Library Drawings Collection.

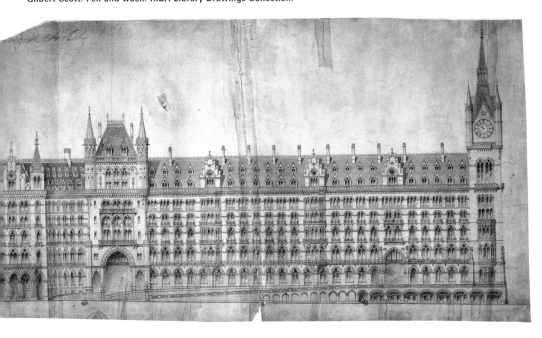

were laid on for special events. The famous travel agent, Thomas Cook, claimed to have transported 165,000 people to the Great Exhibition between May and October 1851. By 1900 an average person made 30 railway journeys a year and the railways had become part of everyday life. They brought about a revolution in transport and communications that remains one of the most remarkable legacies of the Victorian period.

51. *Design for the Great Hall, Euston Station, London*, 1846–9. By Philip Hardwick. Pen and wash. RIBA Library Drawings Collection.

52. *The Railway Station*, 1862. By William Powell Frith. Oil on canvas. © Royal Holloway and Bedford New College.

opulent restaurants (such as Spiers and Pond), alongside popular cafés (such as the Lyons chain), West End theatres and concert halls (including the Westminster Aquarium and The Empire, Leicester Square), and established pleasure gardens (Cremorne or Rosherville). Concerns such as these provided suitable and largely 'respectable' venues for displays of fashionable taste and social interaction that might previously have taken place within a more domestic context.

A proliferation and fast turnover of fashionable styles also ensured that the social signals given out by dress became increasingly complex as the century wore on. At the onset of Victoria's reign in 1837 the respectable woman's wardrobe echoed a much narrower conception of idealized femininity. Close-fitting bonnets, sleeves and bodices, heavy skirts and enveloping shawls for

daywear in dull plaids and stripes, with equally tightly boned and layered confections in paler whites and pastels for evening, bespoke the gentle submission of the 'angel in the home' – that domestic paragon to which most genteel women aspired (see 4:27). By the 1860s the opportunities afforded by new technologies had introduced bright synthetic dyes, showy sewing-machine-made accessories and the extraordinary lightweight support of the wire crinoline (and later the bustle) to the middle-class wardrobe. In this manner the expanding horizons offered by consumer culture dictated a more

53 *The Oxford Galop*, about 1861. Music cover by T. Packer depicting the interior of the Oxford Music Hall, London, opened in 1861. Colour lithograph. VAM Enthoven Collection.

54 *The Young Widow*, 1877. By Edward Killingworth Johnson. Significant moments in people's lifecycles were marked by the adoption of specific costumes and social habits, which also drew the attention of astute businessmen, from funeral directors to department-store managers. Here the roles of bride and widow have followed each other too quickly for comfort. Watercolour and gouache. VAM E.808-1959.

assertive display of fashionable products (*see 4:5*). Like her mastery of the domestic interior, the housewife had to learn how to use the decoration of her body as a sign of her family's prosperity and good standing. Individual elements of the wardrobe increasingly came to be associated with the specific rituals of respectable life-patterns, so that a woman with pretensions to society might be expected to change several times in the course of a day. This effect found its most concentrated form in the intensified clothing regulations applied to christenings, weddings and deaths in the family. The forbidding strictures of mourning dress reconciled the commercial acumen of crêpe and jet retailers with a supposed rejection of worldly concerns. This was a tension that reflected the opposing forces of display and morality inherent in fashion itself and in attitudes towards feminine culture generally.

If a tightening of the rules was necessary to ensure that an engagement with the dangerous world of fashion did not lead to immorality, then their loosening could also be a sign of the heightened sensibility of the fashion consumer. Echoing the trend towards aesthetic interior decoration, the emergence of 'counter-cultural' modes of dressing from the 1860s and 1870s onwards played an important role in the reordering of clothing habits for ordinary British men and women that was in progress by the end of the century. Aesthetic dress was partly a means of self-identification for those members of the metropolitan upper-middle classes who associated themselves with bohemian pursuits and with progressive political sensitivities, and partly a response to the unhealthiness and the perceived ugliness of contemporary fashionable style. But it introduced a real notion of freedom and common sense into the British wardrobe, with its 'natural' colours, 'tasteful' historicist inspiration and unrestrictive cut. It was, however, mercilessly lampooned at the time. *Punch* offered a typically wry take on what it saw as the absurdities of the

55 *I Can't Stand Mrs Green's Mother*, about 1878. Music cover by Alfred Concanen. The variety and expressive characteristics of consumer culture raised their own problems, not least the potential for conflict that the adoption of new fashions and domestic routines carried between generations and social classes. Colour lithograph. VAM Enthoven Collection.

trend in a poem published in 1882 to coincide with a joint exhibition of the Rational Dress Society and the Healthy and Artistic Dress Union:

> Note robes there for rinking, and gowns for tea-drinking,
>
> For yachting, for climbing, for cricketing too;
>
> The dresses for boating, the new petticoating,
>
> The tunics in brown and the trousers in blue.
>
> The fabrics for frockings, the shoes and the stockings,
>
> And corsets that ne'er will the figure compress:
>
> But in the whole placeful there's little that's graceful
>
> And girlish enough for a Rational Dress!

Masculine clothing had benefited from a more 'rational' design since the end of the previous century. Yet despite the apparent simplicity and uniformity that the respectable male wardrobe seemed to offer, the acquisition and use of its content were just as complex as its female counterpart. With different styles of coat for a variety of professional and leisured contexts and a whole range of accessories, from sticks and gloves to shirts and hats, shopping for men's fashion was a serious business. It called on the skills of tailors, hosiers, outfitters, hatters and shoemakers to furnish a complete suit of clothing. Such was their competence at the top end of the market

56 *A Private View of the Royal Academy*, 1881. By William Powell Frith. The apparent constraints of mainstream fashion were challenged by champions of aesthetic dressing. At the Royal Academy disciples of the Aesthetic movement's 'prophet' Oscar Wilde (centre right) gather round him in corset-free outfits of muted colours and medieval inspiration. Oil on canvas. Private collection.

WALKING IN THE ZOO

SUNG WITH DISTINGUISHED APPLAUSE BY

THE GREAT VANCE

ENT. STA. HALL.

"WALKING IN THE ZOO, WALKING IN THE ZOO,
THE O.K. THING ON SUNDAY IS THE WALKING IN THE ZOO;
WALKING IN THE ZOO, WALKING IN THE ZOO,
THE O.K. THING ON SUNDAY IS THE WALKING IN THE ZOO,"

WRITTEN BY

MUSIC BY

HUGH WILLOUGHBY SWENY ESQ & ALFRED LEE

LONDON. C. SHEARD, 192. HIGH HOLBORN, W.C.

that English tailoring became synonymous with quality throughout the world. Underlying this was a theory of 'gentlemanliness', which bound the 'correct' usage of the male wardrobe to a celebration of moral rectitude, physical endeavour and aesthetic 'good form'. This notion ensured that though a man's dress appeared to reject the ephemerality of fashion, it remained a key indicator of his place in society and his attitude to culture. In its more adventurous forms – for example, when the dapper evening suit was taken up as a badge of belonging for cosmopolitan playboys and dandies in the 1890s, or when the relaxed, sporty lounge suit started to break down the stuffiness implied by morning and frock coats in the same decade – masculine fashion offered a universal template for modern dressing. Women rapidly took up its adaptable components, like the washable shirt and the tailored suit, to form a wardrobe more suitable to the expanded life circumstances of the New Woman in the new century. Like other physical aspects of Victorian life, the man's suit proved to be a flexible barometer of cultural change. Its development illustrated how accomplished nineteenth-century consumers were at reconciling the material plenitude of modern life with their social and emotional needs.

58

57 *Walking in the Zoo*, about 1870. Music cover by Richard Childs. Music-hall stars like 'The Great Vance' provided dapper models of masculine fashion and refute the idea that Victorian men were uninterested in issues of sartorial style. Colour lithograph. VAM Enthoven Collection.

58 *An English family taking tea on the lawn*, about 1900. By an unknown photographer. By the turn of the century many consumers could enjoy a wardrobe that was relatively unconstraining, adaptable to modern pursuits such as cycling, and associated with social, sexual and political emancipation. VAM E.2283:6-1997.

POTTERS
DARWEN

CHAPTER 5

What was new?

JOHN STYLES

1. Novelty

Innovation fascinated the Victorians. Human inventiveness in the fields of technology, art and fashion seemed to have spawned an unprecedented variety of new things. Looking back in 1898, the *Popular Science Monthly* reflected that, 'as the nineteenth century draws to a close, there is no slackening in that onward march of scientific discovery and invention which has been its chief characteristic'. Not that innovation was universally acclaimed. Despite the enthusiasm for the new – and sometimes for the fantastic – that could be found in the ever-more numerous popular magazines, the unceasing tide of innovation unsettled many Victorians. Nowhere was this unease more marked than in design and the decorative arts. Critics complained that public taste had come to be dominated by a wilful striving merely to be different, an aesthetic restlessness that paid little heed to notions of beauty derived from the formal principles of the art academies or to Pugin's notion of honesty of construction. 'Novelty, give us novelty, seems to be the cry,' wrote Henry Cole disapprovingly. In 1849 his *Journal of Design and Manufacture* elaborated:

> There is a morbid craving in the public mind for novelty as mere novelty, without regard to intrinsic goodness; and all manufacturers, in the present mischievous race for competition, are driven to pander to it. It is not sufficient that each manufacturer produces a few patterns of the best sort every season, they must be generated by the score and by the hundreds. We know that one of our first potters brought to town last year upwards of a thousand patterns! There are upwards of six thousand patterns for calico-printing registered annually, and this we estimate to be only a third of the number produced . . . One of the best cotton printers told us that the creation of new patterns was an endless stream. The very instant his hundred new patterns were out he began to engrave others. His designers were working like mill-horses.

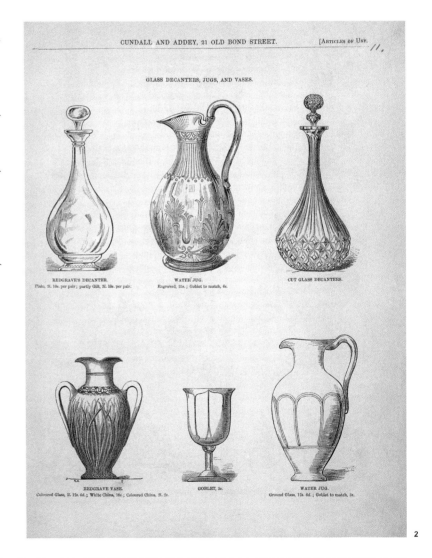

CUNDALL AND ADDEY, 21 OLD BOND STREET. [ARTICLES OF USE.

GLASS DECANTERS, JUGS, AND VASES.

REDGRAVE'S DECANTER.
Plain, 3l. 10s. per pair ; partly Gilt, 3l. 10s. per pair.

WATER JUG.
Engraved, 25s. ; Goblet to match, 6s.

CUT GLASS DECANTERS.

REDGRAVE VASE.
Coloured Glass, 2l. 12s. 6d. ; White China, 18s. ; Coloured China, 2l. 2s.

GOBLET, 3s.

WATER JUG.
Ground Glass, 12s. 6d. ; Goblet to match, 3s.

1 Detail of a wallpaper sample showing a perspective view of a railway station, about 1852. Produced by Potters of Darwen, Lancashire. Wallpaper samples like this in a 'variety of miserable patterns' were included in the exhibit of False Principles in Decoration at the Museum of Ornamental Art, Marlborough House, in 1852. Henry Cole disapproved of this paper because of its false perspective and frequent repeats. Paper, printed from wooblocks. VAM E.558-1980.

2 *Glass decanters, jugs and vases*, 1853. From *A Catalogue of English Art Manufactures, Selected for their Beauty of Design*, published by Cundall and Addey of London, 1853. The objects in the catalogue embodied the principles of good design advocated by Henry Cole and his associates. This page includes a decanter and vase designed by Richard Redgrave, who edited the *Journal of Design and Manufacture* with Cole. Engraving. VAM 37.F.39.

A public appetite for novelties was not, of course, a new phenomenon. The sixteenth, seventeenth and eighteenth centuries had each witnessed the arrival or invention in Britain of multitudes of new things. These innovations were repeatedly accompanied by expressions of concern about the powerful, sometimes irrational grip that new objects exercised on the imaginations and purses of the British population. However, what was distinctive about the nineteenth century was an intense desire to establish an aesthetic distinction between good and bad innovations. This involved drawing an exceptionally stark contrast between 'mere novelty' and 'intrinsic goodness'; between what was described in discussion of design for printed textiles as 'novelty of conception and constant variety of effect' and 'elegance and beauty of execution'. Precisely how this distinction should be defined remained the subject of bitter dispute throughout the Victorian era. Yet these disagreements did little to reduce the appeal of such a distinction as a way of making sense of the tidal wave of new objects that seemed close to overwhelming the human capacity to choose.

By the mid-nineteenth century the growth of national wealth, combined with the accelerating pace of innovation, had brought an unprecedented level of material abundance to broad sections of the population. What and how to choose became the issue of the day, rehearsed in erudite treatises and popular magazines. But it would be wrong to imagine that the Victorian crisis of choice arose simply because innovations in materials and manufacturing techniques made it possible to produce ever-more varied goods at ever cheaper prices.

Many manufacturers undoubtedly believed that by constantly introducing new designs they increased their sales and their profits. Indeed, so great was the pressure on them to differentiate their products by means of design that new laws were introduced between 1839 and 1843 to allow designs to be registered, thereby discouraging piracy. It was at this period too that we begin to observe manufacturers using the names of well-known designers like Christopher Dresser as a selling point. Nevertheless, the crisis of choice cannot be accounted for simply by the desire of businessmen to use design to boost sales. As we have seen, it also reflected the absence of a single, dominant style, at a time when knowledge about historical styles and decorative effects had never been greater or more accessible. It arose out of the competitive anxiety of the ever-increasing population of consumers to use their purchases to improve themselves and their homes. It was fuelled by the conflicting claims about new things with which manufacturers and shopkeepers, designers and critics bombarded the public. Never before had so many people confronted so great a choice of new objects that claimed to be beautiful, but never before had the criteria for making appropriate aesthetic decisions seemed so uncertain.

2. How things were made

The almost miraculous increases in industrial productivity that could flow from the combination of steam power and automatic machinery mesmerized the Victorians. The phenomenon evoked both delight and repulsion, but the powered machine was universally acknowledged as one of the defining characteristics of the age. Yet it was only a narrow range of industries that were utterly transformed by the application of steam power. Indeed, in 1870 transport, in the form of steam ships and railway locomotives, used more steam horsepower than the whole of manufacturing industry. With the exception of cotton and woollen textiles and iron and steel, the impact of steam-powered machinery on British industry was limited before the final decades of the Victorian period. By then, steam was itself beginning to face the challenge of the electric motor as a source of industrial motive power – one that could be applied to small and medium-sized machinery with much more flexibility.

Because powered machinery long remained the exception rather than the norm in many industries, only a small minority of those who toiled in Victorian manufacturing were machine minders. For motive power, much Victorian manufacturing depended on its workers' arms, legs and lungs; for precision, on their keen eyes, steady hands and the almost instinctive

3

3 *The Mill, Saltaire*, about 1853. This sketch of Sir Titus Salt's new worsted mill at Saltaire, Yorkshire, was probably drawn in the Bradford office of its architects, Lockwood and Mawson. It depicts two of the most important mid-19th-century uses of steam power side-by-side – textile manufacturing and the railway. Watercolour and body colour. Salts Estates Ltd.

appreciation of how to combine material and design that came only with long experience. Many industries, such as glass making, used virtually no powered machinery during the whole of the Victorian era. Where it was used, often it was for only one in a long sequence of processes that culminated in the finished product. In the potteries, steam power might be used to mix the clay, but plates, teacups and the myriad other products of the industry continued to be shaped by hand, often on potters' wheels

4 *D'Almaine's Pianoforte Manufactory*, 1830–40. By Thomas Hosmer Shepherd. Pianos are shown being made by hand in this early Victorian factory in Upper Chilton Street, London. Pencil, pen, ink and watercolour. The Museum of London.

5 The upholstery workshop of Harris Lebus, London, 1899. All the work in this late-Victorian upholstery workshop is being undertaken by hand. VAM Furniture and Woodwork Department Library.

CHRISTOPHER DRESSER

Karen Livingstone

As a freelance designer, Christopher Dresser (1834–1904) embodied a new kind of profession. He had a successful studio in London, employing, by 1904, 10 assistants and all five of his daughters. Unusually, Dresser was not a trained architect or professional artist. He studied at the Government School of Design, where he developed an interest in botany and formed influential ideas on nature and ornament from Owen Jones and other prominent lecturers. He began his career as a botanist and lecturer, publishing several books on design, until he started to work full-time as a freelance designer from 1862.

Dresser's inspired approach to marketing his work ensured that his business was successful and that he is remembered as one of the most prolific designers of his age. He toured the country visiting major trade outlets and manufacturers, securing lucrative contracts and selling his designs. His publications – and ventures such as the Art Furnishers' Alliance, with a shop on Bond Street – were intended to promote his work and influence manufacturers. Dresser was one of the earliest designers to have his commercial work accredited to him and his signature marked on the manufactured object. By the height of his career, his name had come to represent a guarantee of 'art value', forcing him to complain in 1875 that some retailers had started to use his name to sell goods that he had not designed.

Like other designers, Dresser looked to non-European sources for inspiration. Rather than imitating historical styles, he created original forms, such as an earthenware vase with a yellow glaze, drawing on sources as diverse as Chinese and ancient Peruvian pottery, which he knew from visits to the British Museum. He visited Japan in 1877 and wrote extensively about what he saw there, consolidating an appreciation of Japanese art and design that was to inform much of his subsequent work.

Dresser's idea of design was utilitarian, aesthetically pleasing and available to a wide buying public. He is notable for responding to new markets and exploiting the properties and manufacturing processes of cheaper materials like electroplate. His most advanced theories on design, such as the correct position of a handle on a teapot, so that it could be lifted without strain and poured without dripping, are set out in publications including *The Principles of Decorative Design*. This approach to function and design as applied to industrial manufacture distinguishes Dresser as one of one of the most exceptional designers of his time.

6. *Christopher Dresser*, about 1861. *Carte de visite* photograph. The Linnean Society of London.

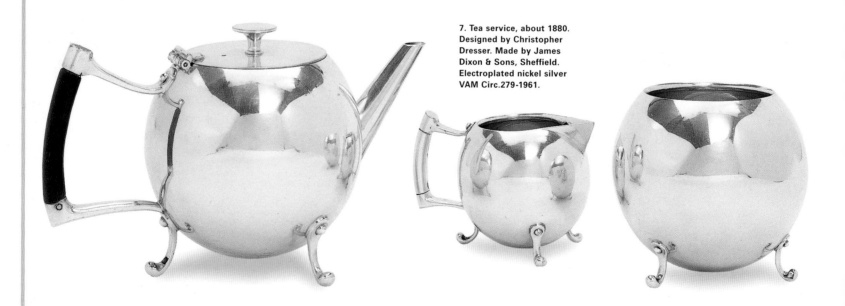

7. Tea service, about 1880. Designed by Christopher Dresser. Made by James Dixon & Sons, Sheffield. Electroplated nickel silver VAM Circ.279-1961.

8. Chair, 1880–3. Designed by Christopher Dresser. Made by Chubb and Co. for the Art Furnishers' Alliance, London. Ebonized and gilded mahogany. VAM W.35-1992.

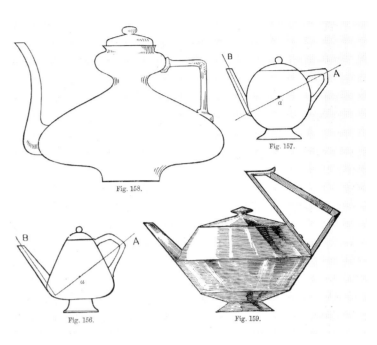

9. Detail of an illustration showing the correct position of handles, from *The Principles of Decorative Design*, 1873. By Christopher Dresser. VAM 58.C.8.

10. The ethnographical galleries at the British Museum showing Peruvian pottery as Christopher Dresser would have seen it, 1880s. The British Museum.

11. Vase, about 1892–6. Designed by Christopher Dresser. Probably made at the pottery of William Ault in Swadlincote, Derbyshire. Earthenware with coloured glaze. [h. 22.1cm]. VAM C.27-1971.

12

that were themselves turned by hand or foot. Even where machines like lathes were powered by steam, as in some branches of the furniture and the metal trades, the quality of the finished product owed everything to the skill of the worker. 'Steam,' it was pointed out in 1850 in the *Morning Chronicle*, was, under such circumstances, 'only the motive power, for a man must still be employed to "turn"'. Dependence on skilled hand labour meant that British high-design goods were far more vulnerable to foreign competition than staple products like iron or cotton textiles, whose production relied on steam-powered machinery.

There were a number of reasons for the limited extent to which steam power was applied in Victorian manufacturing. One was the abundance of cheap, skilled hand labour in a country with a long history of industrial work and a rapidly growing population. Another was the visual intricacy of so many consumer goods and the constant, rapid changes they underwent to satisfy the Victorian love of novelty. Often it was cheaper for a manufacturer to employ workers whose hand skills were admirably flexible than to invest in cumbersome, expensive machines that were difficult to adjust to new product lines. 'In Birmingham,' the publisher Charles Knight observed in 1846, 'the adjustments required by the ever-varying tastes and wants of the age can be effected only by men's fingers.' Similar comments continued to be made up to the end of the century.

It would be wrong to dismiss this phenomenon simply as the survival of antiquated hand skills in those circumstances where steam power could not be profitably applied. The coming of the steam engine did not stifle inventiveness in the hand industries. Indeed, Victorian capitalism created many more hand skills than it destroyed. In workshops across the land, new hand techniques were constantly being developed, accompanied by the use of new materials and novel ways of organizing work, all of which could bring about significant reductions in the cost of hand-made goods. It is worth remembering that the 300,000 panes of glass which covered that acclaimed symbol of Victorian

13

12 *A Pottery Shop*, mid-19th century. By Alfred Morgan. A depiction of work in the 19th-century pottery industry; though highly idealized, it indicates the predominance of hand processes. Oil on canvas. VAM E.1632-1989.

13 *The Pen Grinding Room*, 1851. From the *Illustrated London News*, 22 February 1851. Women workers in the factory of Messrs Hinks, Wells and Co. of Birmingham, steel-pen manufacturers, grind pen-nibs on machines turned by power from a steam engine. Large-scale manufacturing of steel-nib pens was an innovation of the 1830s. Specialized machines, both hand- and power-driven, were developed to make them. Wood engraving. VAM P.P.10.

14

15

modernity, the Crystal Palace of 1851, were all blown by hand, employing a new technique introduced by Messrs Chance Brothers of Smethwick in the West Midlands. In terms of volume and standardization, this was a kind of mass production, but emphatically not one that required the powered production lines and automatic machine tools that came to define mass production of the twentieth century.

Even where steam power played virtually no part in the manufacturing process, the scale of enterprise could be huge. In the 1880s the plant of Sowerby's Ellison Glass Works Limited at Gateshead in County Durham was the largest pressed-glass manufactory in the world. It employed nearly 1,000 workers, producing vast quantities of decorated drinking glasses, decanters, salt cellars, cake and fruit dishes, plates and a variety of objects in opaque glass. The Sowerby's works was not as big as the largest integrated textile factories, like Titus Salt's worsted mill at Saltaire outside Bradford in Yorkshire, with its 3,000 employees. Nevertheless, Sowerby's and a number of other pressed-glass works employed considerably more workers than the average textile mill. At Sowerby's each employee worked an eight-hour shift, making up to 1,200 tumblers a day. Yet this work was all performed on hand-operated presses that

16

14 Advertisement for Sowerby's Ellison Glass Works Limited, 1890. From *The Pottery Gazette and Glass Trade Review*, 1 September 1890. The advertisement for this Gateshead glass-pressing firm includes a panoramic view of the works and an illustration of some of its products. Engraving and letter-press. VAM PP.25.A.

15 Plate, 1887. Made by Sowerby & Co., Ellison Glass Works, Gateshead. Press-moulded glass was a perfect medium for commemorative pieces, like this plate, produced for Queen Victoria's Golden Jubilee. Pieces could be produced quickly and in large quantities from a single mould. Pressed glass. VAM Circ.716-1966.

16 Celery vase, 1887. Made by Sowerby & Co., Ellison Glass Works, Gateshead. This type of ornamental glass with moulded decoration was inexpensive and enjoyed a large market both at home and abroad. Pressed glass. VAM C.263-1987.

were themselves a nineteenth-century innovation. Glass pressing originated in the United States in the 1820s and was introduced into Britain in the 1830s. It enabled decorative glassware to be produced at a much lower cost than the slower and more skilled method of blowing the glass to the required shape and then decorating it by diamond cutting. Steam power was not applied until 1894, when Sowerby's introduced their own patent steam pressing process.

The pace of work at Sowerby's Gateshead plant was not set by the remorseless turning of the belt drives that transmitted power from steam engine to machines in a typical Victorian textile mill. But we should not therefore assume that the men who worked the glass presses at Gateshead laboured any less intensively than their counterparts in the textile factories of Lancashire and Yorkshire. The pace of their work was driven by piece rates – payment by results. A degree of skill was involved, but each worker had to perform a specialized task over and over again at a fast enough pace to earn an adequate day's pay. This pattern – monotonous, highly specialized and often physically demanding work, driven at a hard pace – could be found not just in the larger plants using hand machinery, but in many smaller Victorian workplaces that served the insatiable public demand for decorative goods of all kinds. Indeed, Victorian workplaces tended, in the main, to be small and in 1899 the average British workshop employed only

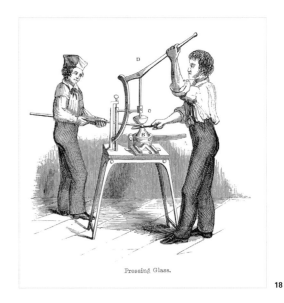

Pressing Glass.

18

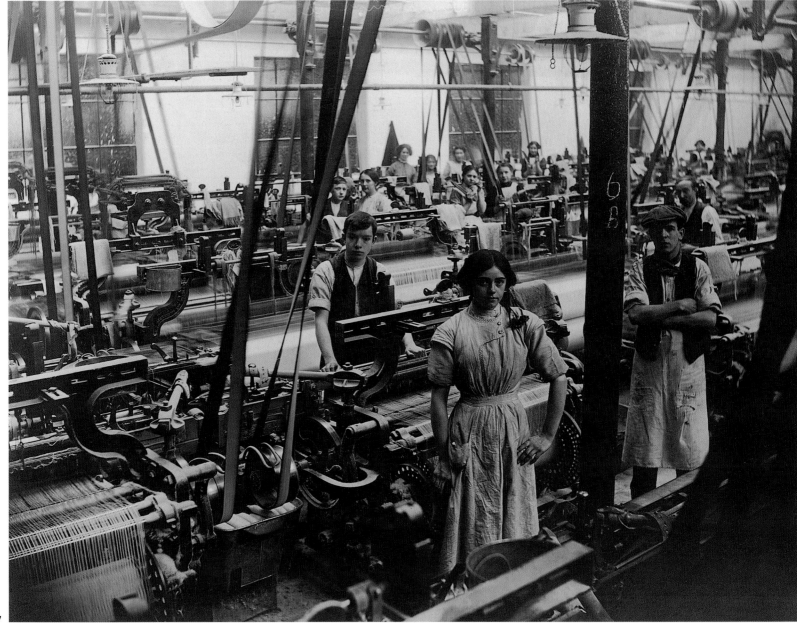

17

29 male employees. By that date, even the largest British industrial plants, in steel making, ship building, locomotive building and armaments, were small by American or German standards. And of course there were many workers, especially women, who worked on their own account at home, or in tiny garret workshops, the notorious sweatshops where seamstresses laboured for 12 hours a day, paid by the shirt or the frill.

When critics like John Ruskin and William Morris attacked the capitalist division of labour for degrading workers and depriving their work of creativity, they had in mind this pressured, monotonous hand work as much as the machine-paced labour of those who toiled in the steam-powered factories. Morris himself was, of course, from 1881 the owner of a manufactory at Merton Abbey in Surrey, on the outskirts of London, which used exclusively hand techniques and employed more than 100 workers. He enjoyed a reputation as an excellent employer who paid well and encouraged his workers in their skills. Nevertheless in most respects conditions at Merton Abbey were

20

not so different from those at many other Victorian workplaces where paternalist employers strove to provide good conditions for their workers, as far as commercial competition would allow. Titus Salt's textile factory at Saltaire was one of the most famous examples of such paternalism. Most of Morris's workers at Merton Abbey were paid on a piecework basis, 'according to the custom of their trade'; their working day was not noticeably shorter than elsewhere; and hand processes were used to give Morris the artistic control over his products that he felt was essential, and not to provide the workers with creative self-expression. Morris himself regretted that these conditions fell far short of his own socialist-medieval ideal, which was fully realized only among small groups of often affluent Arts and Crafts enthusiasts. But conditions at Merton Abbey reflected the pressures that commercial competition forced on the most paternalist of employers, even those like Morris who cornered a niche market among the extremely well-off.

20 Block-printing chintzes at William Morris's Merton Abbey works, early 20th century. Illustration from Morris and Co.'s catalogue, *Printed Linens and Cottons*, about 1912. VAM Textiles and Dress Department Library.

19

17 The weaving shed at John Butterworth and Sons, Dale Mill, Waterfoot, Lancashire, about 1900. The belt drives transmitted power from the steam engine to the looms. Lancashire County Library, Rawtenstall Local Studies collection.

18 *Pressing Glass*, 1849. From *Curiosities of Glass Making* by Apsley Pellatt, 1849. The engraving depicts an early hand-operated glass-pressing machine. A gather of molten glass (B) is dropped into the mould. The man operating the lever then lowers the metal plunger (C) into the mould to shape the glass. Wood engraving. VAM 89.J.50.

19 *The Sempstress*, 1846. By Richard Redgrave. Redgrave was inspired by Thomas Hood's poem, 'Song of the Shirt', especially the lines 'Oh! men with sisters dear, Oh! men with mothers and wives, It is not linen you're wearing out, But human creatures' lives.' Oil on canvas. The Forbes Magazine Collection, New York.

21

3. New materials

A flood of new, improved and often cheaper materials had a profound effect on Victorian design. The introduction of substances like linoleum (invented in 1860 and used for floor coverings), celluloid (invented in 1862 and used for combs, cutlery handles and shirt collars) and the cheap steel that resulted from the inventions of Henry Bessemer in the 1850s and replaced iron in many of its uses, hugely expanded the repertoire of materials from which existing types of object could be made. Consumers appreciated the superior functional properties that new materials could offer, such as improved durability or greater ease of cleaning, as well as the widening of choice. But enlarging choice in this way simply intensified the pre-existing quandary as to the appropriate form and decoration for such objects. When a supremely malleable and easily ornamented material like papier mâché came into vogue for furniture, as it did in the early Victorian years, the design critics were horrified at the results.

Increasingly it was from the laboratory that new materials emerged in the course of the Victorian era, the products of systematic research involving the chemical reformulation of geological and biological substances. Fundamental scientific research did not sweep the board – linoleum, for instance, consisted simply of a combination of linseed oil with resin and cork dust, applied to a woven backing of cotton or flax. Nevertheless, laboratory-based research came to be regarded as the most effective way to generate major innovations, although the discoveries that emerged from the laboratory were not always those that had been envisaged. A prime example of a serendipitous scientific discovery was synthetic dyes.

22

---

21 Sardine fork with a celluloid handle, late 19th century. Fork, electroplated nickel silver, engraved and beaded; handle of celluloid. VAM M.32-2000.

22 Linoleum, 1875. Designed by William Morris. Manufacturer unknown. Printed Corticine floor covering. VAM Circ.527-1953.

23 *The Fashions. Expressly designed and prepared for the Englishwoman's Domestic Magazine*, December 1860. By Jules David. Engraved and printed in Paris by Lamoureux and J. De Beauvais. The new aniline dyes were ideally suited to producing fabrics in the purple and red colours depicted here. Hand-coloured lithograph. VAM E.267-1942.

COAL TAR DYES.
SPECIMENS OF FABRICS DYED WITH
Simpson, Maule & Nicholson's
COLORS.

Concentrated Regina Purple.

Concentrated Violet with a little Roseine.

Phosphine. *Roseine.* *Regina Purple.* *Violet.*

Phosphine. *Printers Roseine.* *Regina Purple.* *No 2 Violet.*

No 1 Blue. *Blue.* *No 2 Blue & Violet.* *Concentrated Printers Roseine.*

SPECIMENS OF FABRICS DYED WITH
Perkin & Son's Colors.

Before 1856 virtually all dyes came directly from natural (mainly vegetable) materials: blues from indigo, reds from madder and cochineal, weld yellows from the wild mignonette. In that year William Perkin, the 18-year-old son of an east London builder, was a student at the Royal College of Chemistry, recently established in London under Prince Albert's patronage. Encouraged by the college's director to find a synthetic substitute for the anti-malarial drug quinine, Perkin produced a black tar from aniline and potassium dichromate. It lacked the anti-malarial properties he was seeking, but turned out to be effective as a dye, producing the colour that became known as aniline purple or mauve. Perkin's new synthetic dye was an immediate success. It was fast and resisted exposure to light. Remarkably, it proved suitable for dyeing silk, the most prestigious material for women's dresses.

Perkin left the college to set up a factory near London to produce the new dye in bulk and make his fortune. His raw material was the coal tar that was available in vast quantities as an undesirable by-product of the huge industry that manufactured gas from coal. Soon other coal-tar-based synthetic colours were invented, in particular magenta, a vivid red. All these new, synthetic dyes were characterized by an unprecedented brilliance and intensity and were taken up with enthusiasm by British women. Their invention did not create the fashion for crinolines in luminescent, gaudy colours, but certainly encouraged it to ever-greater extremes. 'The exaggeration of the dresses of the ladies or young girls belonging to the wealthy middle class is offensive,' complained Hippolyte Taine, a French visitor to Hyde Park in the 1860s, picking out for particular condemnation 'gowns of violet silk with dazzling reflections' and 'gloves of immaculate whiteness or bright violet'. 'The glare is terrible,' he concluded.

24

THE FASHIONS Expressly designed and prepared for the *Englishwoman's Domestic Magazine.*

23

24 Coal-tar dyes, 1862. Samples of aniline-dyed cloth from *The Practical Mechanic's Journal: Record of the Great Exhibition*, 1862. Dyed fabric samples on paper. VAM PP.23.E.

FURNITURE

Frances Collard

New materials underpinned many of the major innovations in Victorian furniture. Some were extremely unconventional, such as coal or Derbyshire slate, and were used on a very limited scale; others, like papier mâché and metal, had an enormous impact.

Although used for tables, trays and boxes from the 1770s, papier mâché was not suitable for larger pieces of furniture until the introduction of improved moulding techniques between 1836 and 1851. Sideboards and cabinets, or chairs and sofas that were intended for heavy use, were constructed of papier mâché on a wooden or metal frame. The Birmingham firm of Jennens & Bettridge was one of the largest and most celebrated manufacturers, as illustrated by their stand at the 1851 Great Exhibition. Their innovations included the development of decorative techniques and of papier mâché for ship interiors and railway carriages.

The search for new materials combined with the Victorian interest in home decoration to prompt the introduction of frames, swags and friezes made of moulded leather instead of the conventional carved wood. These were exhibited in 1851 by Messrs Esquilant & Co. of London and were recommended for their cheapness and durability, particularly for the interiors of steam ships. The same techniques were used for leather leaves and flowers applied to the support of a table by Messrs Morant of London.

One material developed by the metal industry but of great interest to furniture makers was hollow metal tubing, made either from brass or from iron and brass. This was particularly important for bed manufacturers, who produced numerous different designs, marketed through illustrated catalogues. Birmingham became such an important centre that by 1875 almost 6,000 beds were being produced every week, half of which were sent for export.

25. Seat furniture designed by Filmer and Son, London. From the *Illustrated Catalogue of the Universal Exhibition*, 1868. Wood engraving. VAM PP.6.B.

26. Wine tray and decanter. Designed by Richard Redgrave for Felix Summerly's Art Manufactures. Tray, originally produced 1847; this example 1865. Made in Birmingham by the firm of Jennens & Bettridge. Papier mâché, japanned, gilded with appliqué of mother-of-pearl. [h. 40cm]. Decanter, 1848. Made in Stourbridge by W. H. B. & J. Richardson. Glass, wheel-cut and gilded. VAM 132-1865, C.108-1992,

27. Rocking chair, 1840–50. possibly made by the firm of R.W. Winfield, Birmingham. Steel tube, japanned and gilded. VAM Circ. 20-1961.

28. *The Hardware Display*, 1852. From *Dickinson's comprehensive pictures of the Great Exhibition of 1851*, 1854 (second edition; first published 1852). Printed and published by Dickinson Brothers, London, 1854. The Jennens & Bettridge stand is on the right. Colour lithograph with hand-colouring. VAM 46.K4.

29. Star of Brunswick table, 1851. Designed and manufactured by Henry Eyles in Bath. Plaque made by Messrs Chamberlain and Co. in Worcester. Table of walnut, carved and with inlay of pollard oak. Plaque of Worcester porcelain. VAM W.40-1952.

Manufacturers of upholstered furniture also benefited from improvements in other trades. Although springs are recorded in upholstery from the mid-eighteenth century, they were not widely used until the 1830s when spiral steel springs became commercially viable, as noted by John Loudon in his *Encyclopaedia of Cottage, Farm and Villa Architecture and Furniture* (1833). The characteristic deep buttoning of Victorian sofas and chairs was dependent on the use of springs and the innovations in design and construction that flowed from their introduction.

30. *Design for a brass bed*, about 1885. Made for Robert Lloyd Crosbie & Co., Birmingham. Pencil, chalk, water and body colour. VAM E.2820-1995.

By the 1870s the British textile industry had almost entirely gone over to the new synthetic dyes, now available across the colour spectrum. They were cheaper than natural dyes, easier to use and, because of their quick-drying properties, especially suited to mechanical roller printing. Between 1868 and 1878 imports of the natural dyestuff madder fell by 90 per cent. Some resisted the change, in particular William Morris, who characteristically felt that 'every one of these colours is hideous in itself, whereas all the old dyes are in themselves beautiful colours'. In the 1870s he set about reviving the use of the old dyeing techniques for his own products, although not without considerable difficulty. Ironically, by this time Britain was lagging behind Germany in the invention and production of synthetic dyes. In chemistry, as in electricity, the Germans proved able to sustain a much more productive relationship between science and industry than the British.

4. New techniques

The rapid pace of innovation in materials in the Victorian era was more than matched by the proliferation of new manufacturing techniques. Steam power became ever more widespread as Victoria's reign proceeded, but it was virtually unknown for whole industries to be transformed from hand production to production by powered machinery at one go. Some new techniques did have a dramatic effect, however. Silver plating by electricity, for instance, patented in 1840 by George Richard Elkington of Birmingham and his cousin and partner, Henry Elkington, invoked an entirely new power source and rapidly transformed a major high-design industry. Within a decade, electroplating had effectively killed off the making of Sheffield plate, the previously dominant technique for plating base metals with silver. But the sudden change brought about by electroplating was unusual. It was much more common for innovation in technique to be an incremental process, often a matter of piecemeal improvements to existing tools and machines or of profound changes in one branch of an industry, while other branches remained untouched. Nor did new techniques necessarily result in dramatic changes in the appearance of the goods they were used to make. The introduction of colour printing by means of lithography in the 1840s did enable books to be illustrated in colour on a scale and with a quality of reproduction that were unprecedented. However, as the introduction of electroplating demonstrates, it was common for new techniques to be introduced with the aim of making existing objects more cheaply or with greater consistency of quality, not in order to change the way they looked. If significant changes in design did sometimes emerge from such innovations, often it was only in the longer term.

31

32

31 Detail of 'Bird and vine' fabric, 1879. Designed by William Morris. Manufactured by Morris & Co. Wool dyed with natural dyestuffs, jacquard woven. VAM T.14-1919.

32 Teapot, 1853. Made by Elkington and Co., Birmingham. Electroplated nickel silver; cast and applied handle with ivory insulators; cast and applied spout. VAM M.239-1984

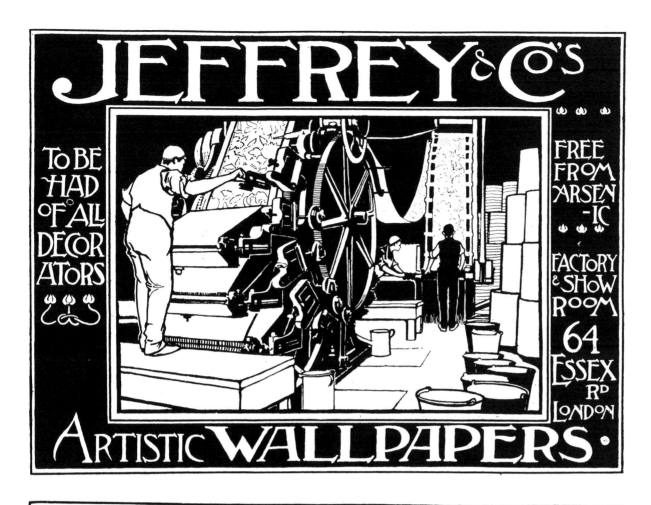

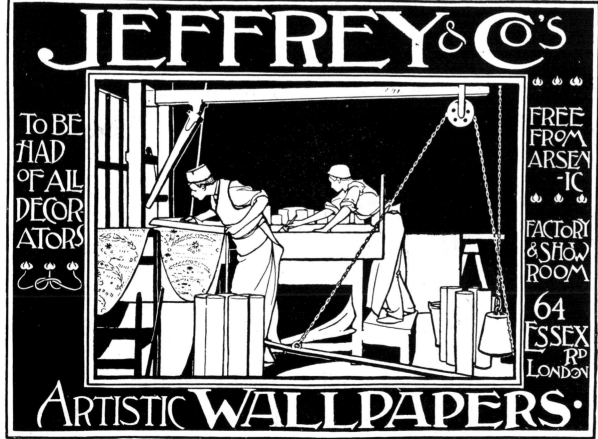

33 Letter-heads of Jeffrey and Co., 1899. These two letter-heads date from the same year and indicate that Jeffrey and Co., manufacturers of artistic wallpapers, used machine printing and hand-block printing side-by-side in their London factory at the end of the Victorian era. Woodblock print. VAM E.42A(2)-1945.

33

Many of these characteristic features of Victorian innovation can be observed in the various attempts to introduce powered machinery into the making of furniture. These took two main forms: firstly, and more successfully, the use of powered machinery in basic preparatory processes like veneer cutting, sawing and planing; secondly, and more ambitiously, attempts to use machines to produce decoration, particularly carved work.

The introduction of machinery into the preparatory processes began in the middle years of the nineteenth century, principally in the large, comprehensive London cabinet-making firms that made the highest-quality furniture in the greatest variety of styles. West End firms like Holland and Sons, Jackson and Graham, and Seddon and Company bought steam engines and equipped their workshops with steam-powered veneer cutters, lathes, vertical and circular saws and mortising machines. The result was a hybrid system of manufacture, which a trade-union report in 1874 described as 'machine-assisted hand production'. Much of the drudgery of preparation was removed. A workman noted in 1867 that 'in shape work, the wood is cut by machinery as well as by hand, and very close and fine, so in cleaning of it only requires the scraper and glass paper to finish'. In the 1880s it could still be said that West End work 'is always supposed to be entirely by hand', although 'the influence of the more rapid methods of machinery begins to make itself felt'. But evidence to a Royal Commission in 1884 pointed out that 'these machines are no drawback to cabinet manufacture. They do all the hard work and still a good cabinet-maker is more essential than ever. The hard work is performed by the machine, but still the work for a good tradesman is left.'

Hand work remained essential because many of the finishing and assembly processes were so difficult to mechanize. For West End firms producing individual pieces of furniture or small batches on a bespoke basis, the highly skilled worker, specialized but capable of adjusting his skills to all kinds of new designs, was indispensable. Of course, West End firms often subcontracted to cheaper East End workshops, which employed less expensive labour, but there the nature of the work (as opposed to the rates of pay) was not necessarily so different. After all, many of the benefits of machinery were available to smaller producers. They could buy materials prepared by means of powered machinery, like veneers, from specialist firms. At the same time they could use small treadle-operated machines, like circular saws and band saws, that did not require steam power. In addition, as Charles Booth's survey of London pointed out in the 1880s, investment in expensive powered machines was inappropriate 'in a market in which workers are so numerous and labour so cheap as in the East End of London'.

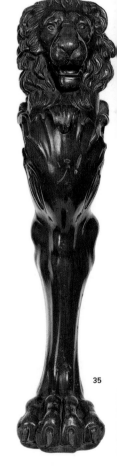

35

34 Cabinet, 1878. Designed by Bruce Talbert; made by Jackson and Graham, London. This cabinet won the Grand Prize at the Paris International Exhibition of 1878. Jackson and Graham was a high-class West End cabinet-making firm with steam-powered machines. Ebony, inlaid with decorative woods and ivory. VAM W.18-1981.

34

View of an INTERIOR as recently embellished with the CARVED WOODS supplied by

THE PATENT WOOD CARVING COMPANY

5 Henrietta Street, Covent Garden.

37

The impact that these innovations had on the way furniture looked is questionable. Steam-powered machinery took over the production of veneers during the first half of the nineteenth century, but this was as much a response to the popularity of veneered surfaces as it was its cause. The paper-thin veneers produced by the rotary-knife cutting machine introduced later in the century were cheaper even than their power-sawn predecessors. But it is not clear that machine veneer cutting always resulted in lower prices for furniture. Sometimes it simply encouraged furniture makers to incorporate more expensive, exotic woods in their products.

Similarly, the use of machinery to make decoration, particularly carved work, did not necessarily result in lower prices. The early years of Victoria's reign saw a boom in the popularity of revived period styles. 'A taste has of late years arisen for carved furniture of the Tudor, Louis Quatorze and Renaissance periods,' reported the *Art Union* in 1841. Wood carving was, however, one of the most time-consuming and expensive methods of decorating furniture. There was thus a powerful incentive to develop machinery that could carve furniture quickly and cheaply. A variety of solutions were introduced, including steam-powered cutting tools that carved out the wood by following the shape of a metal template, and iron moulds, heated red-hot, which burned the decoration into the wood. The cutting machines enjoyed some successes, particularly T. B. Jordan's patent machine, which was used for carved work for the new Palace of Westminster, where large amounts of carving were required. Nevertheless, most carving continued to be done by hand. Not only did machine carving itself need hand finishing, but the cost of constantly preparing new metal templates and cutting tools was prohibitive in a trade where the kind of carved work in demand was constantly changing.

38

35 Machine-carved lion, part of a sideboard, 1848–50. Stamped on the back 'JORDAN'S CARVING WORKS 154 STRAND'. Mahogany, machine-carved with hand finishing. VAM W.7-1967.

36 Carving machines in the factory of Harris Lebus, London, 1899. VAM Furniture and Woodwork Department Library.

37 Frontispiece to *Decorations in Wood*, Part 1, the catalogue of the Patent Wood Carving Company, 1845. The company used the hot-iron mould process to simulate carved woodwork. Lithograph. Bodleian Library.

38 Hand carvers finishing machine-made parts in the factory of Harris Lebus, London, 1899. VAM Furniture and Woodwork Department Library.

BOOK ILLUSTRATION AND BINDING

Rowan Watson

Almost all aspects of book production became mechanized during the Victorian period. By the end of the nineteenth century even the process of sewing printed sheets to make quires into a bookblock was done by a powered machine.

Following the example of Thomas Bewick, wood engraving was revived in the 1830s to allow images to be integrated with text; in the 1840s electrotypes and new presses (the platen and cylinder presses) enabled texts with multiple images to be produced in large print-runs. With the establishment of cheap illustrated magazines, such as *Punch* in 1841 and the *Illustrated London News* in 1842, images became a means of guiding the reader's eye and conveying information in conjunction with the text. A veritable army of designers and engravers emerged to serve the printing industry, but wood engraving was superseded by the advent of photographic methods of reproduction at the end of the

century. By the 1890s magazines for a mass market, selling for just a few pence, contained densely illustrated articles and advertisements.

The exterior of books was transformed by the development of cloths for binding. Until the early nineteenth century books were normally bound in leather. In the late 1820s, however, experiments began with cloth bindings. Cloths were put over prefabricated covers ('case-bindings'), then stamped with lettering, designs and colours, before being attached to the bookblock. From the late 1830s book covers of all kinds, from gift books and annuals to manuals and stories of exploration, could be appropriately decorated in gold and bright colours on coloured cloth, or with a sober image on a magisterial blue or brown, reflecting the gravity of the text. The new technique of lithography was similarly used to provide decorated covers on paper, as well as illustrations. Colour printing based on lithography (chromolithography) was developed by Owen Jones in the 1830s and was widely used commercially from the 1860s, before giving way to mechanical colour printing based on photography.

40. Case binding of green cloth with a design in gold around a coloured engraving on *Lalla Rookh: an oriental romance* by Thomas Moore. Published by George Routledge, 1868. VAM G.28.E.50.

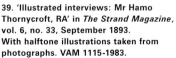

39. 'Illustrated interviews: Mr Hamo Thornycroft, RA' in *The Strand Magazine*, vol. 6, no. 33, September 1893. With halftone illustrations taken from photographs. VAM 1115-1983.

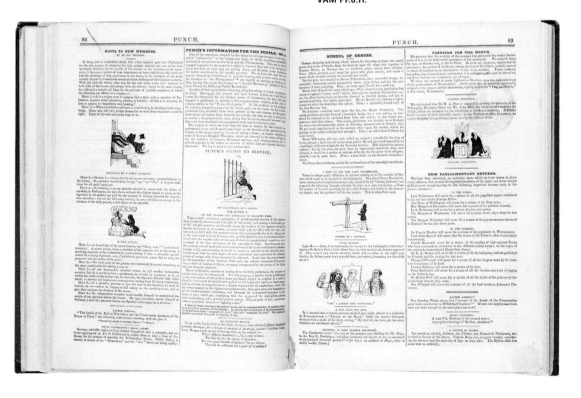

41. Articles with integrated woodcut illustrations from volume 1 of *Punch, or the London Charivari*, 1841. VAM PP.8.H.

43. Cover design by Samuel Luke Fildes for monthly parts of *The Mystery of Edwin Drood* by Charles Dickens, May, July and August 1870. Woodcut. VAM 42.Z.84.

44. Illustration engraved by John Thompson after a design by Daniel Maclise for 'Morte d'Arthur' in *Poems* by Alfred, Lord Tennyson. Published by Edward Moxon, 1857. Wood engraving. VAM 29.Q.48.

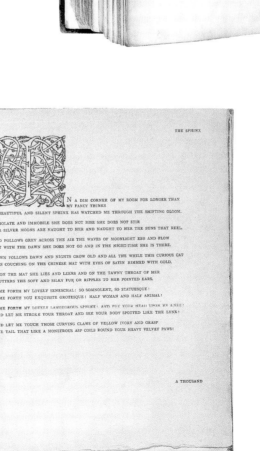

Images on or in books became important for attracting the eye of potential buyers in the bookshop, in the railway bookstall (W. H. Smith was the first in 1848 to see the potential of railway stations for selling as well as distributing books) and in kiosks set up for crowds visiting fairs or major exhibitions. But critics at the end of the century abhorred such displays. In 1899 Gleeson White stated that 'decadence set in with the use of pictures instead of conventional ornament, and the admixture of gold, black and various colours'.

42. Illustration and ornament, designed and engraved by Charles Ricketts for *The Sphinx* by Oscar Wilde. Published by The Bodley Head, 1894. Coloured line-block. VAM L.1524-1902.

45. Cover of *Mrs Brown at the Paris Exhibition* by 'Arthur Sketchley' (George Rose). Published by George Routledge, 1878. Woodcut in three colours. VAM SN.95.0012.

46 Electric desk and wall lamp, 1900. Designed by W. A. S. Benson. Brass. VAM M.957-1983.

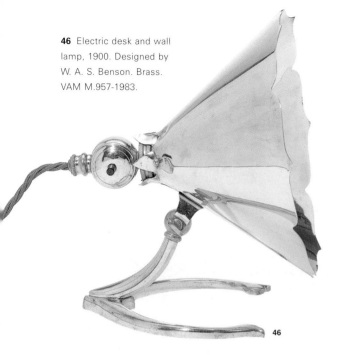

5. New products

If innovation in design and the decorative arts in the Victorian era was sustained and sometimes stimulated by new materials and new manufacturing techniques, it was in new products that it found its most spectacular realization. New products, ranging from the cigarette to the ceramic flushing lavatory, from the exhibition piece to the electric lamp, provided the Victorians with tangible evidence of their own modernity, while throwing up new possibilities and new challenges for design and decoration. The pace of product innovation seemed to accelerate, reaching a crescendo in the last quarter of the nineteenth century, the period that saw the invention of (among other things) the electric-filament light bulb, the phonograph, the motor car, moving

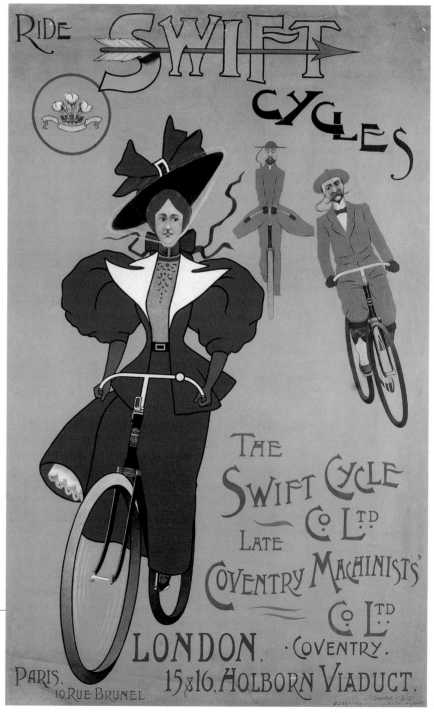

47 Vase, 1862. Figures after designs by Albert Carrier Belleuse. Made by Minton and Co., Stoke on Trent, Staffordshire. Exhibited in London in 1862. This vase is characteristic of the spectacular, technically challenging objects made to win prizes at the new International Exhibitions. Prize-winning pieces were acquired by museums and featured in the advertising of the firm that made them. Bone china, painted and gilded. [h. 95.5cm]. VAM 8111-1863.

49

pictures, the telephone and the safety bicycle. Significantly, only two items in this list of new products originated in Britain – the safety bicycle and the electric light bulb. By the 1870s Germany and the United States, in particular, had become powerful instigators of product innovation, with companies that employed a systematic approach often lacking in Britain.

These new late-Victorian products were widely publicized and stimulated huge public interest. Nevertheless, with the exception of the bicycle, they had limited direct impact on the lives of British people before the end of Victoria's reign, other than for enthusiasts and some of the very wealthy. British homes continued to be lit overwhelmingly by gas; motor cars and the telephone were inaccessible to all but the most privileged; sales of the phonograph were sparse;

and the boom in moving pictures came after Victoria's death. Indeed, it was to take a large part of the twentieth century to develop fully the technical and design potential of the many new products of the late-Victorian years that exploited the possibilities of electrical power and the internal combustion engine.

The new products that became familiar, everyday things before the end of Victoria's reign were principally those invented earlier in the nineteenth century. The list of such products is long and diverse, but two prominent examples – the sewing machine and the railway locomotive – will serve to demonstrate some of the aesthetic challenges posed by the new mechanical objects that so fascinated the Victorian public and Victorian inventors alike.

48 Poster for the Swift Cycle Co. Ltd,
late Coventry Machinists' Co. Ltd,
Coventry, about 1898. Colour lithograph.
VAM E.533-1939.

49 Lord Wimborne in a motor car, 1902.
VAM Picture Library.

The sewing machine was an American invention of the 1850s. It was soon being sold in Britain, where the American firm of Singer became the dominant producer in the later nineteenth century, with approximately three-quarters of the market. In the late 1860s the Singer company set up a factory at Clydebank in Scotland, which became the largest sewing-machine factory in the world. By the 1880s the firm was selling 150,000 machines a year in Britain. Originally designed with industrial production in mind, the sewing machine was soon marketed for family use at home. In the United States, Singer's first machine aimed at the family market was launched in 1858. By 1898 Singer was advertising its 'Improved Family' model in Britain as 'the most perfect machine for family use'. In reality, a good half or more of the machines sold to domestic customers went to poorer households, where women used them to boost family incomes by taking in sewing on a freelance basis or by working at home for firms manufacturing ready-made clothes. But vast numbers of sewing machines were also acquired by middle-class households to enable wives to carry out at least some of the family sewing. The incursion of this mechanical object into the sanctum of middle-class Victorian domesticity posed a question that was almost unprecedented in the nineteenth century, but was to become all too familiar in the next: how to reconcile the look of what was obviously a piece of machinery with the carefully contrived aesthetic of the Victorian middle-class interior?

The manufacturers of sewing machines were well aware of the problem they faced in domesticating their mechanical product. When the Singer company introduced its 'Family' machine in the United States in 1858, it promoted it as 'a machine of smaller size, and of lighter and more elegant form; a machine decorated in the best style of art; so as to make a beautiful ornament in the parlour or boudoir'. As this promotional statement suggests, domesticating the sewing machine did not usually entail any attempt to disguise entirely its mechanical nature (unlike that other and much older piece of domestic machinery, the clock, which was normally cased). Sewing machines were supplied with polished and sometimes ornamented wooden cases, but the machine itself had to be revealed when in use. Nor did domesticating the sewing machine entail a wholesale departure from the look of the early industrial sewing machine. Like much Victorian industrial equipment, early sewing machines for industrial use were customarily provided with some ornament. The solution at which firms like Singer arrived for their domestic machines involved adjusting their appearance in ways that drew on other, existing objects considered attractive and appropriate in the domestic setting.

50 'Arm and Platform' sewing machine, 1875–92.
Designed and manufactured in London by Edward Ward.
Iron and steel; ironwork enamelled with decoration in
the Greek style. VAM Loan: Science Museum: 101.

51 Singer 'New Family' sewing machine, second half of the 19th century. Designed and first produced in 1865 in the United States by the Singer Manufacturing Company of New York. Iron, steel and wood; ironwork enamelled with decoration in the rococo style. Science Museum, London.

52

The basic structural iron components of all sewing machines were finished in black japanned stove enamel. This was necessary to protect the ironwork, but also provided a lustrous appearance. The metal working parts were brightly polished. In those machines intended for domestic settings, the structural iron components were cast in light, elegant curves, sometimes with moulded ornament; the black enamel that coated the iron parts was always decorated with elaborate ornamental details, usually in gold. Neo-rococo was the chief decorative style employed throughout much of the second half of the nineteenth century, but in an age of stylistic eclecticism other styles also

flourished. This mode of decoration imitated the practice, well established since the eighteenth century, of coating a variety of small metal objects for the home with painted japanned ornament. In particular, it mimicked the appearance of the lacquered papier-mâché furniture, trays, writing boxes and other domestic objects which were so popular between the 1840s and 1860s, and were themselves often targeted at the female consumer. The ornamental details on sewing machines were almost identical to those on papier-mâché objects, down to the occasional use of mother-of-pearl inlay, much prized by middle-class consumers but deeply disapproved of by the design reformers. Significantly, the aesthetic formula developed for the domestic sewing machine – black enamelled metal surface, brightly polished metal parts, lining and ornament in gold – subsequently became the model for the decorative treatment of those many new mechanical objects for home, office and leisure use that appeared later in the nineteenth century, including the phonograph, the typewriter and the bicycle. It was to remain the dominant aesthetic for such objects into the mid-twentieth century.

53

52 Work box, about 1850. Made by Jennens and Betteridge, Birmingham. Papier mâché, japanned. VAM W.150-1919.

53 Typewriter, about 1875. Designed in the United States by Christopher Latham Sholes, Carlos Glidden and Samuel Soule between 1866 and 1873. Made in the United States by E. Remington and Sons, Ilion, New York. The machine is shown with the decorative front panel removed. Iron and steel, with decorated enamelled casing. Science Museum, London.

THE PHOTOGRAPH

Mark Haworth-Booth

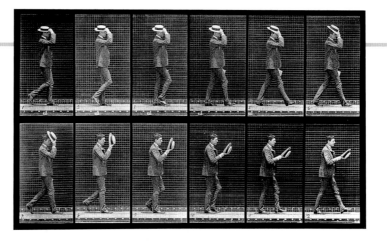

54. *Man Taking off His Boater*, 1887. Plate from *Animal Locomotion*, by Eadweard Muybridge. Collotype. VAM 558-1889.

A man as old as the century is looking from the window of his Paris hotel in the early 1840s. He is one of the first photographers in the world and is enchanted by what he sees – and what his camera can seize. The boulevard below is dusty and hot. His gaze zooms into details: 'they have just been watering the road, which has produced two broad bands of shade upon it, which unite in the foreground, because, the road being partially under repair (as is seen from the two wheel barrows, &c., &c.), the watering machines have been compelled to cross to the other side'. He glances at 'the forest of chimneys' on the horizon and marvels that each one is perfectly

recorded 'for, the [camera] chronicles whatever it sees, and certainly would delineate a chimney-pot or a chimney-sweeper with the same impartiality as it would the Apollo of Belvedere'.

The man is William Henry Fox Talbot, FRS, inventor of positive/negative photography, and he has just said something of profound importance about his invention. First announced in 1839, it swept the world and

remains in use in the present digital era. Few people 'got' photography in its first decade, except as a way of taking astonishingly fast and accurate portraits (using the French daguerreotype system of photography, also announced in 1839).

Photography progressed much as computers did in the later twentieth century, both being initially the preserve of boffins, then of the scientifically inclined, the financially privileged

55. Plate II from *The Pencil of Nature*, 1844. By William Henry Fox Talbot. Calotype. VAM R.1.

56. *Horatio & Colin Ross & Old David Dear Fishing at the falls of Rossie*, April 1848. By Horatio Ross. Daguerreotype. VAM PH.245-1946.

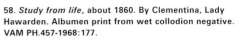

58. *Study from life*, about 1860. By Clementina, Lady Hawarden. Albumen print from wet collodion negative. VAM PH.457-1968:177.

and sometimes the artistically adventurous. Both inventions gradually transformed the world about them, as technical improvements encouraged their take-up for ever broadening purposes. Photography's new standard of authenticity led to the growth of studios, run on factory lines, producing stereoscopic images for home entertainment, portrait miniatures and souvenir views. Both cameras and computers lost their imposing physical bulk and uncertain performance, achieving ease of use and trim, consumer-friendly designs. Both, of course, became essential tools of modern society.

By the end of the nineteenth century photography was in the hands of everyone and was being used for everything. It became as dashing, convenient and fun as that other new craze – cycling. However, it still held the world in the vice of meticulous, enthralled vision celebrated by Henry Talbot as he looked out of that Paris window.

57. Photograph from a family album, 1898. By an anonymous amateur. Platinum print. VAM E.2283-1997.

59

If the sewing machine illustrates the way in which the appearance of a new mechanical object was adapted for use in the home, then the Victorian railway locomotive shows how the imperatives of corporate business shaped the look of another new and, in this case, very public mechanical object. The earliest railway locomotives of the 1810s and 1820s were diverse in appearance. It took some time to arrive at the limited range of relatively stable and recognizable types that prevailed from the later 1830s. This was partly a technical matter, but the aesthetics of the railway locomotive were an issue almost from the start. As early as 1827 – just two years after the opening of the first passenger railway – George Stephenson, the father of British railways, and his locomotive-building son Robert were 'endeavouring to reduce the size and ugliness of our travelling engines'.

The solution they came up with – concealing the cylinders, the crucial and most ungainly working parts, underneath the boiler – delighted the renowned engineer of the Great Western Railway, Isambard Kingdom Brunel, who wrote in 1838, 'lastly let me call your attention to the appearance – we have a splendid engine of Stephenson's, it would be a beautiful ornament in the most elegant drawing room'. Among the elements that were so pleasing were the harmonious side-view, achieved by the use of a large central driving wheel with smaller supporting wheels on either side, combined with strong horizontal forms and the balanced verticals of the chimney and the firebox. In motion, there was no evidence of the functioning mechanism, other than the turning of the wheels. This elegance of composition, which had parallels in the carefully contrived aesthetics of British horse-drawn coaches,

---

59 'Wylam Dilly', 1862. This early railway locomotive was built by William Hedley in 1813 for use at Wylam colliery in Northumberland. It was photographed in 1862 when finally taken out of service. National Railway Museum, York.

60 'Jenny Lind', 1847. An engineering drawing of the 2-2-2 locomotive 'Jenny Lind', designed by David Joy and built by E. B. Wilson's Railway Foundry, Leeds, West Yorkshire, in 1847. Pen and ink and colour wash. National Railway Museum, York.

61 'North Star', 1837. An engineering drawing of the Great Western Railway's 2-2-2 locomotive North Star, designed and built by R. Stephenson and Co., Newcastle-upon-Tyne, in 1837. Pen and ink and colour wash. National Railway Museum, York.

60

combined with the use of neo-classical forms for chimneys, domes and the like, was taken up in many of the locomotives designed at this time. In the 1840s, for instance, the famous 'Jenny Lind' locomotives made by the Leeds firm of E. B. Wilson had fluted safety-valve covers and domes that derived in form and ornament directly from neo-classical architecture.

These aesthetic criteria persisted, and indeed were amplified, as locomotives became bigger and more sophisticated in the second half of the

nineteenth century. But as the century wore on, the look of British railway locomotives came increasingly to diverge from that of their foreign counterparts. This became dramatically obvious at the great international exhibitions. The British considered that their locomotives were uniquely beautiful and they were clear about the reasons. *Railway News*, commenting on the locomotive displays at the Paris Exhibition of 1889, praised the 'magnificent specimens of English locomotives, and their grand simplicity and repose compare from an English point of view very favourably with the complicated external appearance of the continental exhibitors'. The same criteria were invoked by British critics when the Midland Railway was obliged to buy locomotives from the American Baldwin company during an engineering strike in 1897. 'The ungainly assemblages of iron, etc. that will do duty on the Midland Railway as a goods locomotive' have arrived, reported *The Railway Magazine* in 1897. 'So far as appearances go, no connection can be made between the neat engines designed by Mr Johnson for the Midland Railway and the uncouth machine "made in America".' The contrast was real enough, as is clear from a comparison between one of the Baldwin

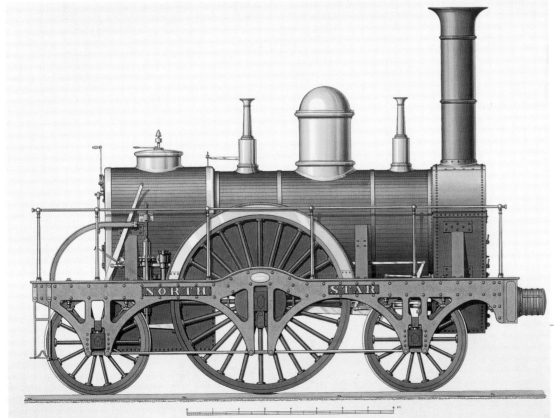

61

locomotives – all exposed cylinders, cranks, pipes and valves – and a sleek Midland Railway locomotive with a similar wheel arrangement.

S. W. Johnson's locomotives for the Midland Railway exemplify the distinctive aesthetic that was so prized in Britain and, indeed, often admired abroad. The terms used by the press to describe his most praised design, the single driving-wheel express locomotives that won the Grand Prize at the Paris Exhibitions of 1889 and (in modified form) 1900, were neatness, harmony, compactness, grace, clean lines, beauty of outline and elegance and symmetry in design. What was being identified here was the British stress on proportion in the overall form of the locomotive, on smooth surfaces without applied decoration, on harmonious combinations of flowing curves and straight lines, and on an overall lightness of appearance enhanced by the use of colour and lining. These were all features that had their roots in the aesthetics of the locomotives of the 1830s and 1840s and, before that, in the design of horse-drawn coaches. In contrast to foreign locomotives, in Britain mechanisms were concealed or simplified to achieve a smoothness of line and a minimum of exposed moving parts. By these means the designers of British railway locomotives created a glamorous impression of speed combined with ease. It expressed their locomotives' mechanical efficiency, without having to reveal it.

The distinctive appearance of British locomotives in this period was in large part a consequence of the way British railways were organized. The technical differences between British and foreign locomotives were not decisive. In Britain, in contrast to much of continental Europe, railways were privately owned and competed on many of their routes. And from the 1850s most came to set up their own locomotive works and employ a chief designer. On the continent and in the United States railways normally bought locomotives off the shelf from independent manufacturers. In Britain, therefore, locomotive design had a unique potential to become an element in competition between railway companies. Locomotive styling was accorded a priority that it rarely enjoyed elsewhere. Along with carriage liveries, staff uniforms and insignia, it became a means of identifying and differentiating between railway companies. The design of each company's most glamorous pieces of equipment had become a means of enhancing its corporate identity.

★

The first half of the twentieth century witnessed a universal reaction against Victorian high design, particularly against its fondness for ornament. But the British railway locomotive reveals a different aspect of Victorian design, one that explored the expressive potential of new technologies and new materials. Far from being at odds with twentieth-century developments, this was a theme that would fundamentally shape design in the twentieth century. European modernist designers of the new century espoused an idealized machine aesthetic. American industrial designers developed novel ways of styling mechanical objects to encourage sales and express corporate identity. In their obsession with being modern, both repudiated Victorian ornament. Nevertheless, both owed a profound debt to the Victorian legacy of technological and corporate design.

62 Midland Railway locomotive no. 673. This 4-2-2 locomotive was designed by S. W. Johnson and built in 1897 at the Midland Railway's Derby works. It was this class of locomotive that won the Grand Prize at the Paris Exhibitions of 1889 and 1900, and was described in the press as 'the very beau ideal of symmetry and grace'. The locomotive is shown as restored at the National Railway Museum, York.

63

64

63 Midland Railway locomotive no. 2510, about 1900. This 2-6-0 locomotive was built in the United States in 1899 by Burnham, Williams and Co. at the Baldwin Locomotive Works, Philadelphia, and exported to Britain. Midland Railway Company photograph. National Railway Museum, York.

64 Midland Railway locomotive no. 1757, 'Beatrice', about 1890. This 4-4-0 locomotive was designed by S. W. Johnson and built in 1886 at the Midland Railway's Derby works. It won a Gold Medal at the Royal Jubilee Exhibition at Saltaire, Yorkshire, in 1887. Midland Railway Company photograph. National Railway Museum, York.

Chronology of Events and Publications, 1837-1901

DATES	POLITICAL EVENTS	DESIGN, ART AND SCIENCE	PUBLICATIONS
1837	Death of William IV, accession of Queen Victoria	Government School of Design, London, founded	
1838		London–Birmingham railway opens	
1839	Parliament rejects first Chartist petition	Daguerrotype announced	*Art Union* (later the *Art Journal*) founded
1839–42	War with China		
1839, 1842, 1843		Design Copyright Acts	
1840	Queen Victoria marries Albert of Saxe-Coburg-Gotha	Rowland Hill introduces the postage stamp Building of the new Palace of Westminster, London, begins	
1841			A. W. N. Pugin, *The True Principles of Pointed or Christian Architecture* *Punch* founded
1842–5			Owen Jones, *Plans, elevations, sections and details of the Alhambra*
1842	Parliament rejects second Chartist petition		
1843			Thomas Carlyle, *Past and Present*
1844		The first telegraph line in England is laid	
1845	Irish famine begins	Building of Osborne House, Isle of Wight, begins	Benjamin Disaeli, *Sybil*
1846	Repeal of the Corn Laws		
1847	'Ten Hour' Factory Act	Felix Summerly's Art Manufactures founded	Charlotte Brontë, *Jane Eyre* Emily Brontë, *Wuthering Heights*
1848	Chartist demonstration, Kennington Common, London	Queen Victoria's first visit to Balmoral	Karl Marx and Frederick Engels, *The Communist Manifesto*
1849		Building of All Saints' Church, Margaret Street, London, begins	John Ruskin, *The Seven Lamps of Architecture*
1849–52			Henry Cole's *Journal of Design and Manufactures* published
1850		Building of Mentmore Towers, Buckinghamshire, begins *The Germ* publishes Pre-Raphelite ideas Isaac Singer produces the first practical sewing machine in the United States	Charles Dickens, *David Copperfield*
1851		Great Exhibition in Hyde Park, London	John Ruskin, *The Stones of Venice*
1852		Museum of Ornamental Art, London, founded	*The Englishwoman's Domestic Magazine* founded
1853		Building of Leeds Town Hall begins	
1854			Coventry Patmore, *The Angel in the House: The Betrothal*
1854–6	Crimean War fought against Russia		
1855			Anthony Trollope, *The Warden* *Daily Telegraph* founded Elizabeth Gaskell, *North and South*
1856		Henry Bessemer's steel-making process invented William Perkin prepares the first aniline dye Celluloid first synthesized by Alexander Parkes	Owen Jones, *The Grammar of Ornament*
1856–60	War with China		
1857	Indian Mutiny	Manchester Art Treasures Exhibition Science Museum, London, founded	
1858	Japan opened to foreign trade		
1859		Frederick Walton invents linoleum Building of the Foreign Office, London, begins Philip Webb designs Red House, Bexleyheath, for William Morris	Charles Darwin, *On the Origin of Species* Isabella Beeton, *Book of Household Management* John Stuart Mill, *On Liberty*
about 1860		The cigarette invented	
1860		London University establishes degrees in science	
1861	Death of Albert, Prince Consort	HMS *Warrior*, the first all-iron warship, completed Morris, Marshall, Faulkner & Co. founded	Charles Dickens, *Great Expectations* *The Queen* founded Ellen Wood, *East Lynne*
1862		International Exhibition, South Kensington, London	
1863		William Whiteley opens his shop in Bayswater, London Football Association established in London	Charles Kingsley, *The Water Babies*
1864		Building of the Albert Memorial begins in London First underground railway opened in London	
1866		The Atlantic telegraph cable is laid Amateur Athletic Club (later Association) founded	

DATES	POLITICAL EVENTS	DESIGN, ART AND SCIENCE	PUBLICATIONS
1867		Building of Manchester Town Hall begins	
1868	Second Reform Act	Building of the Midland Hotel, St Pancras Station, London, begins	Charles Eastlake, *Hints on Household Taste*
	Trades Union Congress founded	C. L. Sholes patents the typewriter in the United States	
		Building of Cardiff Castle begins	
1869	Suez Canal opens	Building of Cragside, Northumberland, begins	Matthew Arnold, *Culture and Anarchy*
			The Architect founded
1870		Building of Eaton Hall, Cheshire, begins	
1871	Bank Holidays introduced	Rugby Football Union founded	*The House Furnisher and Decorator* founded
			Charles Darwin, *The Descent of Man*
1872		Bradford town hall completed	George Eliot, *Middlemarch*
1873			*The Art-Workman. A monthly journal of design for the artist, artificer and manufacturer* founded
			Christopher Dresser, *Principles of Decorative Design*
1875		Trades Marks Act	*Myra's Journal of Dress and Fashion* founded
1876	Queen Victoria declared Empress of India	Alexander Graham Bell patents the telephone in the United States	Agnes and Rhoda Garrett, *Suggestions for House Decoration in Painting, Woodwork and Furniture*
		Building of Bedford Park, London, begins	
1877		Society for the Protection of Ancient Buildings founded	E. W. Godwin for William Watt and Co., *Art Furniture*
		Thomas Edison invents the phonograph in the United States	
		All-England Lawn Tennis Championship first played at Wimbledon	
1878		Joseph Swan demonstrates the electric light bulb	Lucy Orrinsmith, *The Drawing Room*
		Electric street lighting introduced in London	Thomas Hardy, *The Return of the Native*
		Development of Gilchrist-Thomas steel-making process	
1879		First London telephone exchange opens	
1880			Robert Edis, *Decoration and Furniture of Town Houses*
1881		William Morris establishes his Merton Abbey works	W. S. Gilbert and Arthur Sullivan, *Patience*
		Natural History Museum, London, opens	*The Journal of Decorative Art* founded
			Mary Eliza Haweis, *The Art of Decoration*
1882		Electric trams begin to operate in London	Walter Hamilton, *The Aesthetic Movement in England*
		A. H. Mackmurdo founds the Century Guild	
		Building of William Burges's Tower House, London	
1883		Arthur Liberty opens his department store in London	
		Patents, Designs and Trademarks Act	
1884	Third Reform Act	Art-Workers' Guild founded	
		Hiram Maxim invents the automatic machine gun	
		Lewis Waterman invents the fountain pen in the United States	
1885		John Starley introduces the Rover Safety bicycle	W. S. Gilbert and Arthur Sullivan, *The Mikado*
		Karl Benz develops the first petrol-engined motor vehicle in Germany	
1886		Colonial and Indian Exhibition, London	
		John Everett Millais, *Bubbles*	
1887	Queen Victoria's Golden Jubilee	Art and Crafts Exhibition Society founded	
1888		C. R. Ashbee founds the Guild of Handicraft	Jane Ellen Panton, *From Kitchen to Garret. Hints for Young Householders*
		John Dunlop patents the pneumatic tyre	
1890		William Morris establishes the Kelmscott Press	
1891			William Morris, *News from Nowhere*
			Thomas Hardy, *Tess of the D'Urbervilles*
1892		James Dewar invents the vacuum flask	George and Weedon Grossmith, *The Diary of a Nobody*
1893			*The Studio* founded
1894		Lumière brothers invent the cinematograph in France	*The Yellow Book* founded
1895	Trial of Oscar Wilde	The National Trust founded	Oscar Wilde, *The Importance of Being Ernest*
1896		Guglielmo Marconi patents wireless telegraphy	*Daily Mail* founded
1897	Queen Victoria's Diamond Jubilee	Building of Glasgow School of Art begins	*The House* founded
1898		C. F. A. Voysey's Broadley's, Cartmel, Cumbria, built	
1899		South Kensington Museum renamed the Victoria and Albert Museum	
		Felix Hoffman invents aspirin for the Bayer company in Germany	
1899–1902	South African Boer War		
1900			*Daily Express* founded
1901	Death of Queen Victoria, accession of Edward VII		

Design and the Decorative Arts: A Select Bibliography

1. Introduction

Auerbach, J. A., *The Great Exhibition of 1851: A Nation on Display* (1999)

Berg, M., *The Machinery Question and the Making of Political Economy, 1815–1848* (Cambridge, 1980)

Briggs, A., *Victorian Cities* (1963)

Briggs, A., *Victorian People* (1965)

Cannadine, D., *Class in Britain* (1998)

Cannadine, D., *The Decline and Fall of the British Aristocracy* (1990)

Checkland, S. and O., *Industry and Ethos: Scotland, 1832–1914* (1984)

Collini, S., *Public Moralists. Political Thought and Intellectual Life in Britain, 1850–1930* (Oxford, 1991)

Davis, J. R., *The Great Exhibition* (Stroud, 1999)

Denvir, B., *The Late Victorians: Art, Design and Society, 1852–1910* (1986)

Fraser, W. H., *The Coming of the Mass Market, 1850–1914* (1981)

Harris, J., *Private Lives, Public Spirit: Britain 1870–1914* (Oxford, 1994)

Hilton, B., *The Age of Atonement. The Influence of Evangelicalism on Social and Economic Thought, 1785–1865* (Oxford, 1988)

Hoppen, K. T., *The Mid-Victorian Generation, 1846–1886* (Oxford, 1998)

Hunt, J. D., *The Wider Sea: A Portrait of John Ruskin* (1982)

Irwin, J., *The Kashmir Shawl* (1973)

Johnson, P., 'Conspicuous Consumption and Working-Class Culture in Late Victorian and Edwardian Britain', *Transactions of the Royal Historical Society*, 38 (1988)

Knight, F., *The Nineteenth-Century Church and English Society* (1995)

MacCarthy, F., *William Morris: A Life for our Time* (1994)

MacKenzie, J., *Orientalism: History, Theory and the Arts* (Manchester, 1995)

MacKenzie, J. M. (ed.), *Imperialism and Popular Culture* (Manchester, 1986)

MacKenzie, J. M. (ed.), *The Victorian Vision. Inventing New Britain* (2001)

Parsons, G. and Moore, J. R. (eds), *Religion in Victorian Britain* (4 vols, Manchester, 1988)

Pollard, S., *Britain's Prime and Britain's Decline: The British Economy, 1870–1914* (1989)

Porter, A. (ed.), *The Oxford History of the British Empire: Vol. III. The Nineteenth Century* (Oxford, 1999)

Porter, R., *London. A Social History* (1994)

Rubinstein, W. D., *Men of Property: The Very Wealthy in Britain since the Industrial Revolution* (1981)

Said, E. W., *Orientalism* (1979)

Stedman-Jones, G., *Languages of Class. Studies in English Working Class History, 1832–1982* (Cambridge, 1983)

Stedman-Jones, G., *Outcast London: A Study in the Relationship between Classes in Victorian Society* (Oxford, 1971)

Thompson, D., *The Chartists: Popular Politics in the Industrial Revolution* (1984)

Thompson, D., *Queen Victoria: Gender and Power* (1990)

Thompson, E. P., *William Morris: Romantic to Revolutionary* (1977)

Thompson, F. M. L. (ed.), *The Cambridge Social History of Britain, 1750–1950* (3 vols, Cambridge, 1990)

Thompson, F. M. L., *English Landed Society in the Nineteenth Century* (1963)

Walton, W., *France at the Crystal Palace. Bourgeois Taste and Artisan Manufacture in the Nineteenth Century* (Berkeley, CA, 1992)

Wiener, M. J., *English Culture and the Decline of the Industrial Spirit 1850–1980* (1981)

Wright, D. G. and Jowitt, J. A., *Victorian Bradford* (Bradford, 1981)

2. Style

Aldrich, M., *Gothic Revival* (1994)

Banham, J., MacDonald, S. and Porter, J., *Victorian Interior Design* (1991)

Brooks, C., *The Gothic Revival* (1999)

Cooper, N., *The Opulent Eye. Late Victorian and Edwardian Taste in Interior Design* (1976)

Crawford, A., *Charles Rennie Mackintosh* (1995)

Crook, J. M., *The Dilemma of Style. Architectural Ideas from the Picturesque to the Post-Modern* (1987)

Culme, J., *Nineteenth-Century Silver* (1977)

Darby, M., *The Islamic Perspective: An Aspect of British Architecture and Design in the Nineteenth Century* (1983)

Durant, S., *Ornament. A Survey of Decoration since 1830* (1986)

Gere, C. and Whiteway, M., *Nineteenth-Century Design from Pugin to Mackintosh* (1993)

Girouard, M., *The Return to Camelot: Chivalry and the English Gentleman* (1981)

Girouard, M., *Sweetness and Light. The 'Queen Anne' Movement, 1860–1900* (Oxford, 1977)

Greenhalgh, P. (ed.), *Art Nouveau, 1890–1914* (2000)

Head, R., *The Indian Style* (1986)

Jervis, S. and Wainwright, C., *High Victorian Design* (Ottowa, 1974)

3. Who led taste?

Adburgham, A., *Liberty's. A Biography of a Shop* (1975)

Ames, W., *Prince Albert and Victorian Taste* (1967)

Atterbury, P. and Wainwright, C., *Pugin. A Gothic Passion* (1994)

Bell, Q., *The Schools of Design* (1963)

Brooks, C. and Saint, A. (eds), *The Victorian Church: Architecture and Society* (1995)

Burton, A., *Vision and Accident. The Story of the Victoria and Albert Museum* (1999)

Comino, M., *Gimson and the Barnsleys. 'Wonderful Furniture of a Commonplace Kind'* (1980)

Crawford, A., *C. R. Ashbee, Architect, Designer and Romantic Socialist* (1986)

Crook, J. M., *The Rise of the Nouveaux Riches: Style and Status in Victorian and Edwardian Architecture* (2000)

Crook, J. M., *William Burges and the High Victorian Dream* (1981)

Cunningham, C. C., *Victorian and Edwardian Town Halls* (1981)

Davey, P., *Arts and Crafts Architecture. The Search for Earthly Paradise* (1980)

Durant, S., *Christopher Dresser* (1993)

Franklin, J., *The Gentleman's Country House and its Plan, 1835–1914* (1981)

Frayling, C., *The Royal College of Art. One Hundred and Fifty Years of Art and Design* (1987)

Greenhalgh, P., *Ephemeral Vistas. The Exposition Universelle, Great Exhibitions and World's Fairs, 1851–1939* (1988)

Hitchmough, W., *C. F. A. Voysey* (1995)

Jackson, A., 'Imagining Japan: the Victorian Perception and Acquisition of Japanese Culture', *Journal of Design History*, 5 (1992)

Jervis, S., *The Penguin Dictionary of Design and Designers* (1984)

Kaplan, W. and Cumming, E., *The Arts and Crafts Movement* (1991)

Lambourne, L., *The Aesthetic Movement* (1996)

Lambourne, L., *Utopian Craftsmen: The Arts and Crafts Movement from the Cotswolds to Chicago* (1980)

Lubbock, J., *The Tyranny of Taste. The Politics of Architecture and Design in Britain, 1550–1960* (1995)

McCleod, D. S., *Art and the Victorian Middle Class: Money and the Making of Cultural Identity* (Cambridge, 1996)

Mandler, P., *The Fall and Rise of the English County House* (1997)

Morris, B., *Inspiration for Design. The Influence of the Victoria and Albert Museum* (1986)

Parry, L. (ed.), *William Morris* (Woodbridge, 1996)

Physick, J., *The Victoria and Albert Museum. The History of its Building* (1982)

Physick, J. and Darby, M., *'Marble Halls'. Drawings and Models for Victorian Secular Buildings* (1973)

Soros, S. W. (ed.), *E. W. Godwin. Aesthetic Movement Architect and Designer* (1999)

Steegman, J., *Victorian Taste. A Study of the Arts and Architecture from 1830 to 1870* (1970)

Victoria and Albert Museum, *Victorian Church Art* (1971)

Wainwright, C., *The Romantic Interior. The British Collector at Home, 1750–1850* (1989)

Weiner, D. E. B., *Architecture and Social Reform in Late-Victorian London* (Manchester, 1994)

Wolff, J. and Seed, J. (eds) *The Culture of Capital: Art, Power and the Nineteenth-Century Middle Class* (Manchester, 1988)

4. Fashionable living

Adburgham, A., *Shops and Shopping 1800–1914* (1989)

Ashelford, J., *The Art of Dress. Clothes and Society, 1500–1914* (1996)

Bailey, P., *Leisure and Class in Victorian England: Rational Recreation and the Contest for Control, 1830–1885* (1987)

Beetham, M., *A Magazine of Her Own: Domesticity and Desire in the Women's Magazine 1800–1914* (1996)

Benson, J., *The Rise of Consumer Society in Britain, 1880–1980* (1994)

Branca, P., *Silent Sisterhood: Middle-Class Women in the Victorian Home* (1975)

Breward, C., *The Hidden Consumer: Masculinities, Fashion & City Life 1860–1914* (Manchester, 1999)

Bryden, I. and Floyd, J., *Domestic Space: Reading the Nineteenth-Century Interior* (Manchester, 1999)

Burnett, J., *A Social History of Housing, 1815–1985* (1986)

Byrde, P., *Nineteenth-Century Fashion* (1992)

Campbell Orr, C. (ed.), *Women in the Victorian Art World* (Manchester, 1995)

Cooper, N., *The Opulent Eye* (1976)

Crossick, G. and Jaumain, S. (eds), *Cathedrals of Consumption: The European Department Store 1850–1939* (Aldershot, 1999)

Cunnington, C. W., *English Women's Clothing in the Nineteenth Century* (1937)

Curtin, M., *Propriety and Position: A Study of Victorian Manners* (1987)

Daunton, M. J., *House and Home in the Victorian City: Working Class Housing, 1850–1914* (1983)

Davidoff, L., *The Best Circles: Society, Etiquette and the Season* (1986)

Davidoff, L. and Hall, C., *Family Fortunes: Men and Women of the English Middle Class 1780–1850* (1987)

Davidson, C., *The World of Mary Ellen Best* (1985)

Dyos, H. J. and Wolff, M. (eds), *The Victorian City: Images & Realities* (1973)

Feldman, D., and Stedman-Jones, G. (eds), *Metropolis-London: Histories and Representations since 1800* (1989)

Freeman, M., *Railways and the Victorian Imagination* (1999)

Gere, C., *Nineteenth-Century Decoration: The Art of the Interior* (1989)

Gere, C. and Hoskins, L., *The House Beautiful. Oscar Wilde and the Aesthetic Interior* (2000)

Gernsheim, A., *Victorian & Edwardian Fashion* (New York, 1981)

Ginsburg, M., *Victorian Dress in Photographs* (1982)

Girouard, M., *The Victorian Country House* (Oxford, 1971)

Gloag, J., *Victorian Comfort: A Social History of Design, 1830–1900* (1961)

Goodman, A., *Gilbert and Sullivan's London* (2000)

Gow, I., *The Scottish Interior. Georgian and Victorian Decor* (Edinburgh, 1992)

Hoskins, L. (ed.), *The Papered Wall: The History, Patterns and Technique of Wallpaper* (1994)

Kaplan, J. H. and Stowell, S., *Theatre & Fashion: Oscar Wilde to the Suffragettes* (Cambridge, 1994)

Kidd, A. and Nicholls, D. (eds), *Gender, Civic Culture and Consumerism: Middle Class Identity in Britain, 1800–1940* (Manchester, 1999)

Lambert, M., *Fashion in Photographs, 1860–1880* (1991)

Lancaster, W., *The Department Store: A Social History* (Leicester, 1995)

Levitt, S., *Fashion in Photographs, 1880–1900* (1991)

Loeb, L. A., *Consuming Angels: Advertising and Victorian Women* (Oxford, 1994)

Mason, P., *The English Gentleman: The Rise and Fall of an Ideal* (1982)

Merrill, L., *The Peacock Room: A Cultural Biography* (1998)

Morris, R. J. and Rodger, R. (eds), *The Victorian City: A Reader in British Urban History, 1820–1914* (1993)

Muthesius, S., *The English Terraced House* (1982)

Nead, L., *Victorian Babylon. People, Streets and Images in Nineteenth-Century London* (2000)

Newton, C., *Victorian Designs for the Home* (1999)

Newton, S. M., *Health, Art and Reason: Dress Reforms of the Nineteenth Century* (1974)

Olsen, D. J., *The City as a Work of Art: London, Paris, Vienna* (1986)

Rappaport, E., *Shopping for Pleasure: Women in the Making of London's West End* (Princeton, NJ, 2000)

Richards, T., *The Commodity Culture of Victorian England: Advertising and Spectacle 1851–1914* (Stanford, CA, 1990)

St George, A., *The Descent of Manners: Etiquette, Rules and the Victorians* (1993)

Simpson, M. A. and Lloyd, T. H. (eds), *Middle Class Housing in Britain* (1977)

Sparke, P., *As Long As It's Pink: The Sexual Politics of Taste* (1995)

Storch, R. D. (ed.), *Popular Custom and Culture in Nineteenth-Century England* (1982)

Thompson, F. M. L., *The Rise of Respectable Society: A Social History of Victorian Britain 1830–1900* (1988)

Tosh, J., *A Man's Place: Masculinity and the Middle-Class Home in Victorian England* (1999)

5. What was new?

Anderson, P., *The Printed Image and the Transformation of Popular Culture, 1790–1860* (Oxford, 1991)

Ball, D., *Victorian Publishers' Bindings* (1985)

Braithwaite, J., *S. W. Johnson: Midland Railway Locomotive Engineer Artist* (Skipton, 1985)

Briggs, A., *Victorian Things* (1988)

Burman, B., *The Culture of Sewing. Gender, Consumption and Home Dressmaking* (Oxford, 1999)

Bythell, D., *The Sweated Trades: Outwork in Nineteenth-Century Britain* (1978)

Charleston, R. J., *English Glass and the Glass used in England, c. 400–1940* (1984)

Coe, B. and Haworth-Booth, M., *A Guide to Early Photographic Processes* (1983)

Edwards, C., *Victorian Furniture: Technology and Design* (Manchester, 1993)

Forty, A., *Objects of Desire. Design and Society, 1750–1980* (1986)

Glanville, P., *Silver in England* (1987)

Goldman, P., *Victorian Illustration: The Pre-Raphaelites, the Idyllic school and the High Victorians* (Aldershot, 1996)

Hajdamach, C. R., *British Glass, 1800–1914* (Woodbridge, 1991)

Harrison, R. and Zeitlin, J. (eds), *Divisions of Labour: Skilled Workers and Technological Change in Nineteenth-Century Britain* (Brighton, 1985)

Harvey, C. and Press, J., *William Morris. Design and Enterprise in Victorian Britain* (Manchester, 1991)

Haworth-Booth, M., *The Golden Age of British Photography, 1839–1900* (1984)

Haworth-Booth, M., *Photography: An Independent Art* (1997)

Hoke, D. R., *Ingenious Yankees: The Rise of the American System of Manufacture in the Private Sector* (New York, 1990)

Houfe, S., *Fin de siècle: The Illustrators of the Nineties* (1992)

Hounshell, D., *From the American System to Mass Production, 1800–1932. The Development of Manufacturing Technology in the United States* (Baltimore, MD, 1985)

Jenkins, D. T. and Ponting, K. G., *The British Wool Textile Industry, 1770–1914* (1982)

Joyce, P., *Work, Society and Politics. The Culture of the Factory in Later Victorian England* (1982)

Kirkham, P., *The London Furniture Trade, 1700–1870* (1988)

Lattimore, C. R., *English 19th-Century Press-Moulded Glass* (1979)

Levitt, S., *Victorians Unbuttoned. Registered Designs for Clothing, their Makers and Wearers, 1839–1900* (1986)

McLean, R., *Victorian Book Design and Colour Printing* (1963)

More, C., *Skill and the English Working Class, 1870–1914* (1980)

Parry, L., *British Textiles from 1850–1900* (1993)

Ray, G. N., *The Illustrator and the Book in England from 1790 to 1914* (New York, 1976)

Reed, D., *The Popular Magazine in Britain and the United States, 1880–1960* (1997)

Rose, M. B. (ed.), *The Lancashire Cotton Industry. A History since 1700* (Preston, 1996)

Sabel, C. F. and Zeitlin, J. (eds), *World of Possibilities. Flexibility and Mass Production in Western Industrialization* (Cambridge, 1997)

Samuel, R., 'Workshop of the World: Steam Power and Hand Technology in Mid-Victorian Britain', *History Workshop*, 3 (1977)

Schmiechen, J. A., *Sweated Industries and Sweated Labor. The London Clothing Trades 1860–1914* (1984)

Twyman, M., *Printing, 1770–1970: An Illustrated History of its Development and Uses in England* (1970)

Wakeman, G., *Victorian Book Illustration: The Technical Revolution* (Newton Abbot, 1973)

Picture Credits

Index

Page numbers in *italic* refer to both illustrations and to their captions.